ADVANCE

M000074310

switch

Time For A Change

"This is definitely a must-read, inspiring, entertaining and honest look at womanhood, aging and sexuality.

I've read all of Sandra LaMorgese's blogs and they -- like this book -- will inspire women of all ages. I especially dare any woman over the age of 40 to read this book and not feel emboldened and eager to try a new challenge -- asap! Sandra is living proof that you can do anything you want, at any age, and that you can follow your passion no matter what it is. Sandra's journey through life will challenge all your assumptions about middle-aged or 'older' women. Her sexual evolution will make you want to embark on your OWN sexual evolution."

~SHELLEY EMLING, SENIOR EDITOR,
HUFF/POST50

"Based on today's literary climate (Shades of Gray) this is very marketable material.

It is Gray from a woman's perspective. This would appeal to both a male and female audience. Well written. Presented properly as a publisher's pitch! I may have to get a date tonight. LOL!"

~KATHERINE PHELPS, PUBLISHER,
VIVA INTERNATIONALE WOMEN'S MAGAZINE

"Switch is an amazing book, I couldn't stop reading it!
Sandra is a very courageous, strong and talented woman. I know for sure that a lot of people's lives will change after reading this book. They don't have to be the same or do what she did, but they will find their way to a better, happier life. I'm one of them, for sure. After reading *Switch* I feel I can change my life and try to do something different. I was always optimistic, positive, hopeful and smiling in the hardest times, but I never tried to take a different direction or look for something better. It will be different for me now, so thank you, Sandra, so much for letting me live your experience through your book. It was amazing! I lived and felt your entire journey, I'm grateful to you, you're an incredible woman."

~ALLEN B

"Just tell me what can't you do?? I'm hooked!
I'm about 25 pages in and dam girl I'm blown away. WOW!! Doesn't surprise me though. Can't wait to finish!!!!"

~ RA HANNA

"I feel like this book was really empowering for me....
I also loved the message of being authentic and
striving for your own happiness in life. I love it!
I enjoyed it and thus am giving it a four star rating and recommending it! I have recently been reading this authors blog as well and I find it to be enlightening and helpful. I am grateful for having received the chance to read this book!"

~MS. NOSE IN A BOOK, BOOK REVIEWER

"I loved it! I thought it was actually really, really funny and light. And it was really sex positive, which is so great. It's so needed, you know? There's never a book that's about practically applying the tenets of new age spirituality to your life and your day to day and your behavior. Certainly nothing that includes sexuality. Well, nothing that doesn't come off as creepy. I thought it was really original."

~ERIN T

"I finished the book on a flight to the west coast last week.
OMG what an emotional ride for me.
It was great! I got hooked into Sandra's story but also saw my own path thru life in an interesting and different way. I just have too much to say about it."

~PETE P

"Sandra is the perfect guide to a place you always wanted
to know about, but were too scared to visit.
Her well-written narrative is part travel-guide to the world of BDSM and part honest life confessional of a tough, fiercely intelligent woman. The descriptions of the inner working of BDSM subculture and professional dominatrixes are utterly compelling and clearly by an insider. This is not a book written by a reporter on the sidelines and that comes across on every page. Sandra's ability to convey her transformation and ultimate triumph makes Switch a book that has a wide appeal beyond the BDSM community."

~MATT W

"Quite possibly one of the most revolutionary memoirs you'll ever read."
Sandra LaMorgese's *Switch: Time for a Change* is different. Aside from the fact that I really like Sandra, her story about how she how she changed her life post-divorce in her early to mid-50's, especially when it came to dating, sex and sexuality, is personal, powerful and honest, and not just the parts in which she decided to become a Dominatrix at 55.

Aside from getting an inside look into her training and sessions at a Manhattan BSDM dungeon, Sandra's midlife sexual evolution is more than just about spanking, knife play and humiliating grown-ass masters of the universe. It was her way out of getting pummeled by a financial-crushing business blow. It was also part of discovering her sexual side and how it built her confidence in all aspects of her life, including dating.

It's a very thoughtful, mindful, intelligent and very open-minded memoir. I have no doubt that you'll find Sandra the kind of person you'd want to be with or be like."

~BOBBIE MORGAN, A GOOD WOMAN'S DIRTY MIND

"This was a truly wonderful read that should
inspire everyone, not just women,
to not let anything stand in their way of becoming who they truly are! Speaking as someone who has had the pleasure of spending time with Sandra and "Mistress," I can concur that this book is a perfect representation of the woman who authored it."

~JAY K

"I just finished 'Switch' and absolutely LOOOVED it!
Sandra speaks the truth from the heart and we can all take a lesson away from it. You don't have to become a Dominatrix to apply her wisdom to your life. It's about finding your passion and follow it wholeheartedly, not caring about other people's opinion, defining boundaries, not taking any BS, being authentic and true to yourself, not judging and finding out what makes you happy. I can relate to everything you say! Thank you for sharing your journey towards happiness and being brave enough to follow through! The world needs more people like you. You are a true inspiration and I am so happy we met!"

~Monika Werner, Director, Teacher,
Yogini at Bold and Naked Yoga

"Man you gave guts!!"

~Carolynn Mincin,
The Most Unbalanced Woman in Comedy

"Switch" is an erotic journey of self discovery and personal empowerment.
While reading this book, I found myself looking forward to each page and chapter as I learned more and more about myself as a person, through the experiences of Sandra/Vivian. In the end, "Switch" proved to be about the journey each of us is able to take in order to realize our most authentic self. Brilliant, erotic, insightful are just a few words I'd use to describe "Switch."

~Maryam Moshiri O'Connor, Clinical Director
at Utopia Healing Center

It was so refreshing to read about your journey of self discovery. Reminding us to focus on love, not fear is such an amazing life lesson. I could relate on so many levels; your story has inspired me to continue to explore my sexuality and emotional self awareness. I love the connection you make between yoga, meditation, tantric and our sensuality. I was married for over 30 years and found myself suddenly single in my mid 50's. My life had been dedicated to taking care of others, finally it was my "time for a change". I received a message from a guy on a dating site that simply read "I am Dom". Something stirred deep inside and despite my fears, I knew it was something I had to pursue. Recently I met a kinky gentleman who has asked if I could dominate him. My past fears and inhibitions would have held me back but after reading about your transition, my response was 'hell yeah'. From your book I learned that it's essential that I embrace my naughtiness not push it away. You are truly inspirational; thank you on behalf of all powerful and playful women.

~Cheers, Debbie

"I loved 'Switch' –

I bought it as I first came across Sandra on FB and found her posts interesting and funny – thought I'd give 'Switch' a try and was pleasantly surprised and very entertained – it was a down to earth honest account of Sandra's introduction into the world of S & M – not just that, as the reader it certainly knocked my judgements about S & M out the window – it really is a must read – it gives the right amount of detail without going on and on – saying that, it certainly left me wanting more – will wait with anticipation for Sandra's next chapter."

~Tina O

"After reading Switch a couple months ago, I came to realize
that if I want change my circumstances, whether financial
or life changing, it is up to me to make it happen.

Like many of her readers, Ms. LaMorgese was just coming out of
a divorce and was stuck in the boring circle of everyday existence.
She showed me that through meditation and yoga I could build my
self confidence. She also helped me to not be ashamed of my desires
and fantasies and how acting on them can actually empower me. It
has been liberating to talk about my fantasies (with my husband)
which I have always kept private in the past. It is a turn on to him
and things just get better all the time. I would recommend this book
to my friends."

~Jo Anna S

switch

Time For A Change

Cover design and layout: Erin Tyler

Published by EdgePlay Publishing, New York, NY 10018

ISBN: 978-0-9862639-0-3

ISBN-10:0-9862639-0-7

EdgePlay

PUBLISHING

switch

Time For A Change

——— BY ———

SANDRA LAMORGESE, PHD

EdgePlay

PUBLISHING

Contents

Section One
THE AWAKENING

*"It's exhilarating to be alive in a time of awakening consciousness;
it can also be confusing, disorienting, and painful."*

~ADRIENNE RICH

Section Two
THE SWITCH

*"Begin to see yourself as a soul with a body
rather than a body with a soul."*

~WAYNE W. DYER

Section Three

FINDING NIRVANA

"The secret of happiness is freedom, the secret of freedom is courage."

~CARRIE JONES, NEED

FOREWORD

⸙

Right now, our world is sexier than it has ever been. We have
come far from the not-so-good old days of sexuality being
treated as something dirty and taboo, and we're beginning to learn
how to celebrate sex rather than fear it. Though we still have a
long way to go before freedom of sexual expression is a reality for
everyone in our society, we are beginning the important work now
through honest, authentic conversation. We're talking with one
another, asking questions, and telling our stories, and these
conversations are going to change the world.

When we tell each other our stories, we give others the courage to
tell theirs with confidence and pride. When we talk about our own
experiences of overcoming uncertainty, doubt, and other people's
judgmental attitudes, we spread a message of hope and reassurance
that no one is alone in their search for sexual legitimacy. When
we are open with others about our struggles, we open the door to
empathy and acceptance, and we slam the door shut on fear, shame,
insecurity, and judgment. Our stories are powerful tools for social
change, and they are also amazing gifts that we can give to other
members of our community.

I first met Sandra through her work for The Huffington Post, and I
saw a driven and successful woman, full of passion for her career
and for life. She is a woman transformed, and her whole life is now

dedicated to the pursuit of happiness for herself and for others who want to follow in her footsteps.

In Switch: Time for a Change, Sandra shares her incredible journey of transformation from an overworked, unfulfilled, and disillusioned rule-follower to an empowered and deeply happy rebel. Her story is a tale of relentless hope and unfailing courage, but most of all, it is a story of one woman who was brave enough to chase after her dreams alone. She was determined to break down whatever social taboos stood in her way—all without any guarantees of success.

Today, though, her success is clear.

As the CEO of Penthouse Global Media, I am grateful for women like Sandra. It is because of such brave visionaries that the world is getting closer to acceptance of free and unique expressions of sexuality. Every day at Penthouse, we are working toward a future where sexual enjoyment and curiosity are celebrated as healthy and normal. I envision a world where all women have free ownership of their bodies, where all sexual orientations and preferences are welcome, and where all consensual sexual experiences - from the most vanilla to the spiciest BDSM fantasies - are celebrated. This is not always a popular idea - society is still highly conservative when it comes to non-traditional sexual practices, but I for one, have never taken what society says too seriously.

Like Sandra, I didn't enter the world of adult entertainment until later in my career, I knew immediately I had found a home I was comfortable in. The women defied the cliché of "victim." They were smart, funny and insightful about their choices. That is not to say misogynistic content is not easily available. It's available in this genre, on HBO and Showtime, on NBC and CBS. Which is all the more reason that the adult industry, happily, now has a large number of women behind the camera and in the boardroom. Penthouse has always been a leader in open discussions on human sexuality. Most notably through our brands Penthouse Letters and Penthouse Forum. Although it may be surprising at first glance to see a woman own an iconic men's brand, the core DNA of Penthouse has always been crafted for men...and the women they love.

Switch: Time for a Change is exactly the kind of eye-opener we need if we want to shed our shame toward sexuality. Sandra realized that the rules she grew up with were nothing more than chains, holding her back from her true potential. If we want to walk into this kind of sexual and personal authenticity as well - follow her lead, make your own decision instead of letting others make decisions about your bodies, your happiness, and your relationships.

This can be a scary process. Stories like Sandra's give us courage to press on and to stand up for our own happiness and freedom. Through all her struggles, Sandra survived and thrived, and now her inspiring story lights the way as we each figure out how to talk about sexuality and make it our own. Do yourself (and the rest of the world) a favor by joining the conversation.

When we each find the courage to stand up for our own desires, our own fulfillment, and our own joy, we will find the power to dramatically transform our lives. I hope that after reading Sandra's story, you will be inspired to take a chance on true happiness and take part in the sexiest revolution the world has ever seen.

Kelly Holland
Owner and CEO
Penthouse Global Media Inc.
Publisher, Penthouse Magazine

INTRODUCTION

⮪

I t's true. I never thought I'd be working in the most famous bondage, discipline, sadism, and masochism (BDSM) dungeon in New York City. Not to mention that I'd start at the ripe age of 55. If you had told me ten years ago that I would kick a man straight in the balls wearing six-inch heels, blood-red lipstick, black eye shadow, and false eyelashes, I would have kicked you out of my house.

A year prior to my life "switch," I was a lot like you—I was an average, overworked, underpaid, less-than-balanced woman managing a small business and seeking happiness wherever I could find it. The problem was, I couldn't find it. I wasn't even close. I was working 12-14 hour days, seven days a week. I had weekly appointments with an acupuncturist and massage therapist to reduce my stress headaches and agonizing neck and back pain. I rarely socialized, and I was in debt. I never traveled. And my love life? You must be joking.

I thought I was living my dream. I was practicing holistic health care, a field I am very passionate about, and I owned my own wellness studio. I was very grateful to dedicate every day to helping others by educating and inspiring them to maintain optimum health. But there was something missing: my life. As the days, months, and years went by, I listened to my clients telling me their stories of weekends spent at the shore, the parties and family gatherings, the engagements, adventures, and all the wonderful changes in their lives. I was happy for all of them, but I couldn't help wanting the same for myself.

This is the story of how, for the first time in my life, I made decisions from a place of love, not fear. How I came to live in peace by believing the Truth of "When I ask, I will receive."

I live in a perfectly healthy body, am peaceful emotionally and spiritually through practicing yoga, meditation, prayer, jogging, spending quality time with friends, and resting. I wear a $7,000 diamond (the stone of prosperity) around my neck as a show of gratitude and as a reminder of my unlimited prosperity. I nourish my body with organic foods instead of junk food, alcohol, and cigarettes. I work 10 hours a week and dedicate the rest of my time to nature—hiking, rock scrambling, and looking out over the magnificent ocean. Best of all, I am happy where I am right now.

In this book, I share my journey through my dark side to get to the light. I share how I utilize the transmutation of sexual energy, and I map out precisely how becoming a professional dominatrix has allowed me to live the fulfilling and passionate life I always wanted. This book is not rated G. All names of the people on my journey have been changed to protect the innocent— and not so innocent— and all occurrences mentioned are from my personal perspective and memory.

This book will undoubtedly stir up many emotions. That is my hope. For some, this book may bring up feelings of outrage over the way I've bridged the gaps between sexual expression, health and wellbeing, BDSM, God, and spirituality. I suspect many others like me, however, will feel the love, compassion and comfort of hearing the Truth.

I am Mistress Vivian. I am a dominatrix.

THE AWAKENING

*"It's exhilarating to be alive in a time of awakening consciousness;
it can also be confusing, disorienting, and painful."*

~ADRIENNE RICH

Chapter One

WHAT IS SEXUALITY?

—∞∞—

"Sex is something you do; sexuality is something you are."

~ANNA FREUD

T he sedative-laced lotion had worked. I stood over my unconscious patient, who was now hog-tied on top of my table. There was only one way to revive him...and it was going to hurt.

A massage therapist who treated her clients this way would rightfully have her license revoked—prison time might be involved—but I had no fear of professional repercussion. I was a dominatrix and my "unsuspecting patient" was happily paying for the privilege. In the 90-minute power exchange session, we played that I kidnapped him as he was delivering a top secret package to my home. Once my victim was out cold, I tied him up and slapped his face to pull him out of unconsciousness.

I proceeded to threaten him physically and emotionally until he agreed to deliver a fistful of 100-dollar bills to me every week. Once I was satisfied, I released him from the bondage and allowed him to worship and massage my feet.

After the session was over he exclaimed "Mistress, I feel so good right now. Every time I have a session with you, I feel like a rainbow." Four days later he emailed me to share his gratitude for my enthusiasm and energy, which he was still feeling physically and emotionally, and to describe the big smile on his face.

HOLISTIC HEALTH CARE AND SEXUALITY

In the 20 years I worked as a holistic practitioner, I tried to help my clients understand how connected our mental, physical, and spiritual states are. How what we put into our being impacts what our body, mind, and spirit are able to accomplish, and that our health responds not only to fresh water and nutritional foods, but also to our beliefs, emotions, feelings, and the way we think about ourselves and others. My words often fell on deaf ears.

The people who came to my office were typically there to lose weight, explore anti-aging strategies, or to recover from serious illness. It was rare that my clients were motivated by a personal desire to work out, eat healthy, or sleep well. They were there to solve a problem that had gotten out of control—not to explore a new way of life. My clients would listen patiently to my advice, but they rarely left with any new passion for their holistic wellbeing.

If I started talking about Tantric sex, however, their attention would be all mine.

The perfect alignment of body, mind, and spirit is what leads to optimal wellness. And guess what? Being sexual is a huge part of that equation. My clients were intrigued by this turn in the discussion—and why wouldn't they be? We are sexual beings, and therefore sexual curiosity is innate in all of us.

My clients were eager to consider the possibilities in the restorative powers of their sexuality, but they were reluctant to believe that using their sexual force could help create a life filled with happiness and good health. It does almost sound too good to be true. However, I was a living example. My journey into female sexual empowerment and my study of Tantric sex was very organic, and as I saw the transformation working in my life, I knew how powerful it could be for others. These same practices eventually led me to my career as a professional dominatrix and fetishist.

Today, I work with clients who are aware of the emotional, physical, and spiritual healing powers of sexual energy and authenticity. During our sessions together my clients often experience a release of dopamine and serotonin, the brain's feel-good neurotransmitters. These two chemicals are associated with feelings of happiness, tranquility, joy, self-confidence, emotional wellbeing, and motivation. This is why my client felt like a rainbow after our massage therapist roleplay. In addition, the release of the chemical vasopressin compels people toward feeling bonded to one another, which accounts for his affectionate follow-up email four days later.

Physical contact is also meaningful and important in my practice and in my clients' sense of wellbeing. The skin is the largest organ of the body, with millions of receptors right under the surface; receptors that, when stimulated by human touch, can lower our cortisol levels. Long-term high cortisol levels, which are usually a reaction to emotional stress, are associated with low libido, restless sleep, poor digestion, and low immune response. When someone touches our skin, though, through massaging, playing, hugging, hand-holding, or having physical sex, we begin to experience physiological and physical healing.

Mental healing also comes from expressing our sexuality and truly being present in the interaction. When we're 100% engaged with our partner(s) or ourselves sexually, the constant chatter and noise in our minds quiets down, even if the physical activity we're experiencing is intense. Letting go of judgment, expectation, and anxiety in our sexuality brings healing. Focusing solely on the present moment is rejuvenating.

There are ways to reach this state of presence and focus outside of sex, of course. I go rock scrambling and I ride a motorcycle, both of which can be dangerous and potentially fatal if I let my attention wander. When I participate, I have to be completely focused on what I'm doing and fully aware of my surroundings. I can't be thinking about work, the electric bill, a boyfriend, or getting my car to the garage for a tune-up. The activity is intense and demanding, but my mind is—must be—clear. When this happens, I lower my blood pressure, strengthen my immune system, and decrease my emotional anxiety just as much as if I were meditating.

Sexuality is our energy life force. It helps keep us alive, vibrant and connected to the Divine through body and spirit. When we engage sexually with our partner(s) or ourselves, the experience of love and intimacy changes our physical bodies and our spiritual energy, drawing us closer to Universal consciousness every time we open ourselves to the transformative power of sexuality.

With this in mind, just think for a moment about how much time and effort we spend trying to enhance our lives through exclusively external means—chasing others' approval, diet plans, fitness innovations, pharmaceutical drugs, or vacations to make us happy and healthy. We pursue physical solutions and gratification relentlessly, all while our mental and spiritual health decline unnoticed, causing incalculable damage.

I suggest that instead of following every new health trend, we learn to be our own advocates for health and wellbeing. Let's look within in order to discover our own authentic selves and needs and tap into the natural, powerful, healing energies of our sexuality.

SEXUALITY AND MORALITY

I believe having sexual fantasies is normal and healthy. Furthermore, I am sure most of us would indulge freely those fantasies if we didn't have such negative social influences affecting our choices. Much of what we hear from modern society is a constant source of shame and guilt concerning gender-appropriate behavior, sexual experimentation, and the search for authentic and personal sexuality. These external influences may include family members, the media, religion, and culture, and even if we are aware of them, these variables deeply affect how we experience and express sexuality. Perhaps, for example, we accept the common Madonna/Whore dichotomy that oversimplifies sexuality into strictly black and white moral categories. This view of sexuality holds that certain behaviors are good and moral, while others are unquestionably "bad." And, all too often, these judgments of "good" and "bad" don't end with the behavior, but come to define the individual as well.

This way of thinking has to go. When sex is consensual, there should be no rights or wrongs, morally speaking. The BDSM code is "Safe, Sane, and Consensual." It is an agreement that everyone in the room must commit to, and it defines the framework of the fantasy. If the behavior fits within our desires and it makes us happy, then it's all good.

Not every obstacle standing in the way, however, is external. Many (if not most) of the barriers that stand between us and authentic sexual expression come from within, and even if we have strong and healthy physical desires, we all still have to work through what we believe about our gender, body image, orientation, dysfunction, how we participate (or disengage) in sex or masturbation, and many more highly personal variables. We have to ask ourselves, "How do I feel about my sexuality?" Do you feel good about having a strong physical sex drive? Do you enjoy having sex with your partner(s) three times a week? Maybe three times a day? Do you love your body and walk around with as much swagger as a supermodel in Vogue or GQ? Or, do you live in shame and fear of your sexuality? Do you avoid intimacy for long stretches of time? Have you given up on bringing yourself personal pleasure by masturbating? Are you so consumed by the size of your penis, ass, muscles, or waist that you don't feel desirable or worthy? Sexuality is a crucial part of our unique identities, and how we feel about it influences our choices every day. Over time, our attitude toward sexuality has the power to shape who we become.

GENDER, DESIRE, AND SCIENCE

R ecent scientific research suggests that our sexuality begins to develop before we are even born.

Did you know that both male and female genitals come from the same embryonic tissue and are identical in the first stage of fetal development? During the whole first stage, the sex of the fetus remains undetermined. After the first stage, a Y chromosome could produce the hormone testosterone, which would lead to the external and internal sexual differentiation of a male, or an additional X chromosome could prompt production of estrogen, leading to a female.

Some theories espouse that these hormones actually encode our brains before birth—and that the many external factors we experience during childhood development do not determine our sexual and gender identity. Some medical researchers even theorize that our sexual orientation—whether we consider ourselves heterosexual, homosexual, or bisexual—is something that is determined in utero through hormone production. These studies support the theory that sexuality, in its many complex and flexible forms, is hard-wired into our brains.

Over the past few years I've had many clients who say they are transgender and that they wish they were in a position emotionally and financially to undergo gender reassignment surgery. Many people in this situation choose to suppress their true sexual identity altogether, out of shame or fear. Suppression, repression, and denial, though, are not viable long-term solutions, and more often than not lead to self-destruction, guilt, confusion, and self-hatred, as well as physical, emotional and spiritual pain. Others, however, endeavor to explore themselves and their desires, and together, we pursue other forms of authentic and satisfying sexual expression. During our sessions, such a client may take on a feminine role and dress in lingerie, make-up, nail polish, and wigs to help assist in the expression of being female. Often, the only option these clients have for acting and living in a way that matches how they feel inside is through a secret life, and yet they embrace the sexual and emotional outlet of the sessions and are able to feel happy and fulfilled in the end.

THE PRICE OF AUTHENTICITY

I once met an inspiring woman who, after spending 50 years living her life unhappy and unfulfilled as a man, found the courage within to live the rest of her life with authenticity and happiness.

"I knew from the beginning that I was different," she told me. Though Geena had been born with male genitals, she always felt that she was meant to be female. "Even in my earliest memories I was playing with dolls and liking to wear girl's clothing and things," she recalled. When Geena's preferences didn't fade during elementary school, her parents felt that her tendencies were due to a "mental problem" and sent their fourth grader to a psychiatrist.

In spite of the therapy, her feelings never changed. "I remember when girls were starting to grow breasts. I was really envious, but for different reasons from the other adolescent boys. I wanted breasts, and I wanted to be able to dress like the girls. I wanted to be one of them." Geena's mom was supportive and would allow her to stay home from school and dress how she wanted—"As long as I would clean the house that day"—but she was not allowed to leave the house dressed like a girl.

Naturally, suppressing her true feelings for so many years had a negative impact on Geena's self-esteem, self-worth, and identity. She did a lot of drugs to temporarily escape her reality, to find a reprieve from her emotional pain, but they only postponed dealing with the problem and made Geena's mindset even worse.

In everyday life, Geena did all she could to try to be the guy that society expected her to be. She dated women and eventually married. But after 50 years, she just couldn't take it anymore. "I just couldn't live as a guy anymore." She confessed her true self to her wife in March and they were divorced by July of the same year. The decision hurt Geena tremendously. "How would you feel giving up everything? I had to walk away from my life . . . my home, my family, and most of my cherished processions." It created a great deal of bitterness in her family relationships that still continues today.

Through all the turmoil her honesty caused, Geena drew strength from the knowledge that her decision honored her authentic self. "I wanted to be happy. I hated myself, and I was mad at the whole world. I really didn't know why. I just couldn't live as a guy."

The first step of her transition brought intense emotional pain— the next would require her to endure physical pain and financial sacrifice. Removing her beard through electrolysis cost $25,000, then another $10,000 went toward the breast implants that were Geena's birthday present to herself. The "bottom" surgery was $28,000, during which doctors removed the penis and the scrotum and performed painful electrolysis in the bathing suit area. The procedure, called an orchiectomy, severely reduces the body's production of testosterone and involves construction of female genitalia from the existing male parts. Once the penis is removed, the doctors turn it inside out and use it as the passageway of the vagina to maintain the sensitivity there for intercourse. They then cut the scrotum into four pieces to form the labia. At this point in the procedure, Geena experienced her first complication: "One of the skin grafts didn't take." The area is still red and raw and exceedingly painful. The surgery lasted seven and a half hours and the healing process will be a long one.

Amazingly, that was the easy part.

Geena travelled to Philadelphia for facial and cosmetic surgery. "They removed my Adam's apple by cutting three sides of a rectangle around it then shaving it off with some kind of scalpel." Geena had the corners of her chin ground down and an implant put in to create a softer, more feminine shape. The next surgery removed skin from her nose and mouth. Surgeons then began her "facial feminization" surgery. "They cut ear to ear on my hairline and pulled my forehead down. They cut the muscles around my eyebrows then ground eight millimeters off my skull to remove old brow-line." The muscles are just starting to work again there and most of Geena's forehead is still numb. The nerves are just beginning to grow back.

As I listened to Geena's stories—the emotional pain of her divorce, the physical pain of her surgeries, and the constant difficulty of dealing with societal prejudice—I had to ask her, "Is it all worth it?" "People say you have a choice," she answered. "Sure, you have a choice. You can hold a rock over your head, but eventually you have to let it go." The pain that came from letting go of that burden, of finally dropping the rock on her head, was devastating for Geena, but it was the lesser of two evils.

"That's why I'm ready for the next 50 years. Before this change, I could have cared less if I lived or died. I know I'll want to go on until I'm 100."

The question, therefore, becomes: How far are you willing to go to achieve authenticity? Geena denied her authentic self for decades, swimming against the current of what she knew was her truth, before deciding that she was worthy of a life filled with happiness no matter what the fallout. By being honest about who she really was, she lost a spouse and many friends and strained her relationship with her family. Continuing to fight her true nature, however, would have caused Geena to suffer for the rest of her life.

What risks and sacrifices are you willing to make in order to nurture your true nature?

TRYING ON MISTRESS VIVIAN

A s I was deciding to become a professional dominatrix and fetishist, I asked myself, *Can I handle other people's judgmental attitudes about my sexuality? Can I accept another person's sexuality without judgment?* In the end, I decided I could—or at least that I would try. It was a slow process that required me to first deal with my relationship to my own sexuality, and then to practice my free will enough to choose how I wished to express my sexuality.

One conversation that never got old at The Dungeon (the BDSM/ fetish club I used to work in) was sexual preference. It was actually very empowering and freeing to hear a group of women speak openly about their sexuality. Never before had I heard women express with such confidence their gender preferences, curiosities about sex, and interests.

On my second day of work as Mistress Vivian, we sat around the lounge creating my image. I had no clue how I was going to present myself as a *Mistress*, but I knew I wanted to operate with class and dignity. Mistress Deborah chimed in, "I'm going to tell you exactly who you are. You are the sexy cougar, mommy, aunt, school teacher, and so on. You are so sexy, I would fuck you myself, and I don't even like white girls!"

Damn, I'd never heard a woman speak so openly about her sexual preference for the ladies in public! Lesbian, bisexual, straight, formerly lesbian now bisexual, formerly bi now straight—the attitude around The Dungeon is "change happens." In other words, *whatever floated my boat six months ago may not be working for me anymore and that's okay.*

What it boils down to is personal growth, personal progress, and personal choice. To be honest, it was kind of fun flirting with the girls in The Dungeon. And when you think about it, why not? I flirt with heterosexual men with whom I have no intentions of having a sexual affair.

It's incredibly freeing and empowering to be in an environment where your sexuality is not being judged. In fact, it's healing.

Apart from finding the nerve to break (and try to change) society's rules, the hardest part about becoming a dominatrix was mustering up the confidence to talk about it publicly. I knew that by doing so, I'd risk facing both the silent and not-so-silent judgment of others and almost certainly some level of public ridicule. On the other hand, I needed to make a website.

Mistress Vivian needed an online profile as a dominatrix and fetishist, and posting a photo gallery was critical to marketing my brand. If I was going to post pictures of myself in fetish dresses for public consumption, you'd better believe I was going to hit the gym first. For three weeks I trained with my fitness coach to get my body toned for a photo shoot. I've known my trainer for over a decade and I trust her fully, so I felt confident in opening up to her about my secret life as a dominatrix. This was one of my first opportunities to reveal Mistress Vivian to people who had only ever known Sandy.

"Explain it to me," she said. "What is the purpose? I picture you in black leather with a whip in your hand. Are your clients into pain?"

It's a common misperception—a stereotype. And I totally get why. Whenever the media portrays a fetishist or a Domme, as we're called in the industry, she is typically dressed in leather, wearing thigh-high boots and a mean scowl, and covered with tattoos. And while I do own such garments, my look and attitude only scratch the surface of the relationship I have with my clients.

"It's a power and sexual energy exchange. And for the most part, it's not what I'm *doing*, it's how I'm making my client *feel*," I explained. The props and the costumes are there to increase the drama, but that the real play comes from my relationship with my client. "The practice of BDSM involves trust, compassion, love, acceptance, erotica, and surrendering control...That, along with a few necessary beatings," I said, winking at her.

My trainer was curious: How did my transition begin? How did I go from owning a wellness studio to practicing BDSM professionally? Grinning, I began to tell her about an amazing journey that began three years earlier—"I stumbled into this new way of life on the wave of a force so strong that it was impossible for me to ignore. I discovered the emotional, physical, and spiritual healing power of my sexual energy."

Chapter Two

REALIZATION OF POSSIBILITIES

———∞∞∞———

"Sometimes you don't know when you're taking the first step through a door until you're already inside."

~ANN VOSKAMP

My journey started mid-January in 2010. I was sitting at my desk and feeling very excited because an editor from a regional health and beauty magazine was coming to my wellness studio to interview me about the holistic treatments I offered. I looked at the wall to my right, which displayed my degrees and professional certificates, and felt very grateful that all my hard work and dedication was now being recognized with media coverage.

Everything was ready with time to spare, so I decided to check my email. There was one message in particular that I was hoping to see and I wasn't disappointed. I eagerly opened John's email, knowing there was chance it might be of a sexual nature.

My instincts were right.

John and I met online and, after a few weeks of getting to know one another, we decided to meet in the city for a drink and a bite to eat. It didn't take long to discover we had chemistry, and it didn't take John long to make a move on it.

At the time, it had been over three years since my divorce, and I was looking to get back into the dating scene…and I was definitely interested in kickstarting my sex life. After three years of no sex, I felt like all my sexual desires and instincts were gone. It was an unhealthy path that I did not want to continue along. I had finally realized that "all work and no play" is not a healthy lifestyle, and besides, at 53 years old, who was I saving myself for? I was ready to have some fun!

I arrived at the restaurant before John and took a seat up at the bar and ordered a club soda. As I waited, I was feeling really good about my efforts to balance my life and excited about meeting a new guy. John soon arrived, and (thank God) I didn't have any problems recognizing him from the photos he sent. I stood up, we said hello, gave each other a friendly hug and took a seat in a nearby booth.

As soon we sat down John asked "What are you drinking?"

"Club soda" I answered casually.

"Oh no, we need to get you a cocktail. Let's party!" he said with a smile. *Party?* I thought to myself, *I'm not fucking partying. I'll have one glass of wine and that's it.*

"I'll have a wine white" I replied.

Over the next hour John and I discovered that despite our 10 year age difference, we had plenty to talk about. I am into health and fitness, John is into health and fitness. I just bought a motorcycle, John has a motorcycle. I have a son, John has 2 daughters. So, with the conversation going well and the solid chemistry between us, it didn't take long for him to draw closer to give me a kiss on the mouth.

As we kissed, all those feelings that I thought I lost began to surface. I started to get nervous. So, I made a quick excuse to get up from the booth, saying I was going to the ladies room. As I walked away, all I could think about was whether or not John was checking out my ass. When I returned, we finished our drinks and John asked, "Would you like to see my office? It's not far from here."

As the elevator reached the top floor of the office building, my heart was beginning to race and I wanted to chicken out. I started telling myself, "I'm only being sociable. We are not having sex on his desk, a sofa, or anywhere else."

After a tour of John's impressionable office space, we started moving closer to one another and the sparks began to fly! My first reaction was to go with the flow and enjoy the moment, and then the second thought followed, just as strong: *Don't do it! get to know him better!* In those heated moments, my thoughts raced back and forth between "If it feels good, do it!" and "I don't know him well enough to trust him!" What if the immediate sex led to an immediate dismissal on either of our parts? I always hated that. Plus, if I like someone enough to see them again, I love the courtship stage—

discovery, flirtation, and anticipation moving like a dance between us—before taking it to another level. As far as I'm concerned, that's the fun stuff!

In the end, I decided to say good night before things moved in a direction I wasn't sure I wanted. However, I was open to exploring possibilities between us, including sending sexy emails to one other.

A WHOLE NEW KIND
OF STAGE FRIGHT

T he first time John sent me a naughty email I was taken aback. I didn't grow up in the Internet age, so I had no experience with this sort of play. I wasn't really sure if I even wanted a man to talk to me like this via email. As I read how he wanted me to perform oral sex on him and how he was going to fuck me, my first thought was, *Fuck you, pal! Who the hell do you think you're talking to?* But I held my tongue. I went out with John because I wanted to have fun, to try to expand my boundaries, and closing myself off to something new felt like a step in the wrong direction. *Maybe, I wondered, it could be fun to being talked to this way? Maybe, this is exactly what I need?*

Opening up to sexual communication with John reminded me of the way I felt when my acting coach at the Lee Strasberg Theatre and Film Institute in New York City asked me to open up to my sexuality in an improv exercise before an entire class of onlookers. Despite my fears and resistance to becoming vulnerable to others with my feelings, I talked myself into throwing caution to the wind in my first acting class. Why not give it my all and take a risk? What was the point of acting lessons if I planned to hide my uncomfortable emotions as I'd been doing my whole life? This was my opportunity to explore my feelings in a safe environment surrounded by like-minded people.

Our classes began with weird breathing and physical relaxation techniques, followed by a process of visualizing past life experiences to draw up emotion. Once I got into the "zone," I was able to create dialogue to match my feelings. It was clear it really didn't matter what my lines were, but the emotions behind them were what counted. It was effortless to catch onto the "Method." In fact, in some cases it was more difficult to leave the character behind when the scene was over.

I suppose Sam, my acting coach, saw some kind of sexual energy quality in me, and he suggested I tap into it before I started scene work with my partner. His suggestion came 8 years before I started studying the transmutation of sexual energy, so I was not at all comfortable with his suggestion. On the contrary, I felt very intimidated and anxious about the whole idea. *Fuck that*, I was thinking to myself. *I don't want to expose myself that much.* It took more than a few minutes of anxiety, sweating, and words of encouragement, but finally I decided to trust my nerves, and my coach.

I was sitting alone on a hard, cold, metal fold-up chair in front of the entire acting class. I went through a few minutes of relaxation techniques, and then I imagined a hot sexual encounter I'd had years prior. After 10 minutes of sitting in front of everyone, I became physically aroused through my visualization process. My heart started to race, my breathing was becoming heavier, and yes, my panties were wet. Once my coach felt I was ready for my lines, he asked me to open my eyes and start the dialogue.

You could have knocked me over with a feather when I opened my eyes to find a young, sexy, and very attractive black guy sitting across from me instead of my original acting partner. With all of this sexual energy flowing and the huge risk factor of exposing myself emotionally to this hot guy, it was an intense few minutes!

The scene began, and just when I thought was handling my lines well, my acting coach would direct me into an improvisation in which I had to tell this guy how much I wanted to fuck him and what I intended to do to him sexually once I got him alone. I began experiencing such a sense of euphoria that's difficult to describe, and I wasn't alone; the whole class felt it too, and you could have heard a pin drop in the room. From my peripheral vision, I saw that the entire class was at a standstill, eyes wide, and jaws dropped.

I felt that same jaw-dropping euphoria now while I read John's emails.

LEARNING TO LOVE
NAUGHTINESS

⤜⤏

J ohn and I were making the most of the few minutes before the
editor's arrival. We were sending sexy emails back and forth,
writing about John's hard cock and how he imagined sliding it deep
inside me. After three or four naughty messages, I realized I only
had a few more minutes before my guest was supposed to arrive.

"We'd better stop. My interview starts soon and the editor will be
here any minute."

"No, don't stop. Use the sexual energy in your interview!"

...What?!

Instantly though, I found myself intrigued by the idea that I could
somehow use my sexual energy to generate enthusiasm during my
interview. I had heard of other holistic practitioners—such as Reiki
masters—who use energy in their work for healing and creating
balance for their clients, but it was not something I had ever
explored before.

"A few more minutes then," I wrote back.

When the editor arrived, we began with a tour around my wellness
studio. She looked relaxed and curious as we made our way to the

different therapy rooms. As we made our way through the space, I could feel the sexual energy exuding from within me in the form of enthusiasm, confidence, and self-assurance. I wasn't trying to flirt or be sexy, but I was certainly getting my mojo on.

My positive energy had a palpable effect on my guest as I told her about my work and my passion. I could see her own energy lifting as she responded in kind, telling me about her dreams and experiences. We spent hours together in the relaxation room, well beyond our scheduled time, chatting about health, wellbeing, and our opportunities to work together on upcoming projects.

That evening while I closed up the studio, I reflected on how confident I felt in the interview. I thought about my friend John, my sexuality, and how, now more than ever, I wanted to explore my sexual energy in a new way.

FROM COMPLACENCY TO CURIOSITY

M ost of my romantic experience has been as a married person or as a serial monogamist, but quite frankly, I never felt a sense of ease in any of those relationships. There was always an undercurrent of drama, a power struggle. I was always attracted to men who I felt were a challenge, but in actuality, they were unavailable emotionally, physically, or spiritually. Unavailability was something

I'd always known. It defined the relationships I had with my family from an early age, and I spent my life unconsciously seeking to repeat that model.

As I got ready to return to the dating scene in my 50s, though, I decided I was going to break the uncomfortable and unfulfilling lifelong patterns I'd had with men. It was time to stop subjecting myself to an emotional "Groundhog Day" and start living. *After all, I figured, I'm financially independent, full of vitality, my biological clock has stopped ticking, and I just want to have some fun and explore different possibilities.* It was clear to me that if I wanted a different experience in my love life, I had to change the way I thought and felt about myself, dating, relationships, and sex. So, I thought it would be a good first step to simply date and not tie myself to one guy. This, however, presented a challenge. I knew nothing about how to date more than one man at a time.

So the following morning, I Googled it.

Typing "how to date more than one guy at a time" may sound silly, but I've always found that dating even one guy is confusing enough—it was overwhelming to imagine juggling multiple. Is there a protocol? A scheduling system? I didn't know. When I saw the 200 million-plus results pop up on my screen, I dove into my research with glee. I had a hopeful feeling this was going to be fun!

I spent a couple of hours reading all sorts of articles on the subject, including those on men's advice websites and women's empowerment blogs, then I came across an article about younger men dating older women. Here was an idea I could get into. I clicked the link and, lo and behold, I arrived at a dating website for "cougars."

My eyes got wide as I viewed all the lovely profiles of hot younger men seeking to date older women. *Really?* Within five minutes, I had entered my credit card information. *Sign me up!* I thought. I was hooked, I felt alive, and ready to go. *Woo-hoo!*

My curiosity was more than piqued, but I still felt a little naughty at the idea of cruising a dating site of this kind. I reminded myself of my intention: I was looking for a new experience and wanted to start having fun. The profile I set up was pretty normal, vanilla even. In the first section I listed my interests in health and wellbeing, going to concerts, sports, comedy clubs, food and wine, and how I love spending time outdoors. I was honest about the fact that I was over 50. Then in the second section I listed what I was looking for in a guy: "smart, funny, between the ages of 30-40, single, fit, good looking, and seeking fun inside and outside the bedroom." I posted a picture of myself in my ski outfit. I found it hilarious that with all the information I listed about myself and what I was looking for, most of the guys listed only one word in their description or interests. "Fun!"

I nervously wondered if I'd get any responses. I had no idea what to expect, and honestly, I felt a little vulnerable. *Whatever,* I figured, *it's worth a shot.* I clicked to upload my profile information just as one of my scheduled clients arrived for her wellness appointment.

During her treatment, my Blackberry started buzzing like crazy.

For a moment, we both sat and stared silently at my phone. Then I made the snap decision to tell her. She was curious. I accessed my email account right then and there to see what the hell was happening. We realized that the rapid-fire buzzing on my Blackberry was a string of responses to my newly uploaded profile. They were coming in so fast that we weren't able to keep up with them!

The messages from the guys were flirtatious, saying, "I would like to learn more," and "I am interested in getting together," and some were longer, personally written messages. And they just kept coming. "Hey sexy, you wanna chat?"

Over the next week, the whole cougar phenomenon had my head spinning. I'd been on dating websites before, and I'd get a reasonable number of responses within a month, 40 or 50 on average. But after just seven days on this cougar website, I had over a thousand hits! *What the fuck is going on here?* I wondered.

I was so curious about this age differential attraction that I found myself logging onto the cougar dating website every day. Forget about dating more than one guy at the same time—now I had so many options I couldn't keep up! They were short, tall, black, white, Asian, Hispanic, fat, skinny, athletic, couch potatoes, dentists, students, executives, teachers, pimple faced, married, single, or sometimes just fake profiles altogether.

Obviously, I wasn't interested in dating all of them. However, I decided this time not to give any one suitor all my time and attention. I would choose how much time I'd dedicate, depending on the person. In fact, I realized, I could make all the choices I wanted to.

At times, I felt a little pressure to be polite and answer all the emails that were coming in, and sometimes I responded if a guy simply showed sincerity. But some of the profiles were downright ridiculous. Like the guys with their baseball caps turned to the side –DELETE– or if they were 18 –DELETE– or if they lived 3,000 miles away –DELETE– or if it was a photo of them standing next to a keg of beer at a college dorm party giving me the thumbs up –DELETE. Oh, and my all-time favorite, if their profile picture was of their cock or an assortment of full-body shots from their "private gallery." DELETE–DELETE–DELETE! I kept thinking to myself, *Don't these guys realize they're sending their profiles to a grown woman?*

If a profile held my interest long enough, I offered a guy the chance to chat with me, but if he moved to sexual topics too quickly, the conversation was over. A few times I received messages from guys who would simply ask me for naughty pictures of myself so they could jerk off. Nope. One asked for training: "Would you mold me, teach me, use me and train me the way you want?" Not interested. Another skipped the introductions and the small talk altogether, steering our conversation straight to sex. Slow down, cowboy.

I don't want to sound like a prude, because I assure you, I'm not. But this scene was unlike anything I'd ever experienced, and while I was excited, I was also a little disturbed. I felt that many of the guys were pimping themselves, and it didn't exactly feel like dating. Still, it was captivating. My girlfriends and I spent hours checking out profiles over a bottle of wine.

Some of the guys were slick. There's a term I've learned through BDSM known as "topping from the bottom," which refers to when someone *pretends* not to be the one in the power position, while still doing their best to control the entire situation. You know the type: the cool, patient guy. He reels you in slowly and gently, and the next thing you know, BAM! Suddenly you have more naked pictures from the bathroom mirror than you know what to do with.

The sexual energy was certainly there. Naughtiness? No problem. But I didn't feel like I was actually benefitting in any tangible way from my time on the site. There had to be a better way. Sure enough, a light bulb went on. Why not embrace all this naughtiness instead of rejecting it? Why not use my powerful sexual energy to help me shape my life the way I did in the interview with the magazine editor?

LIVING OUT SEXUAL ENERGY

On a typical day, I arrived at my wellness studio in the early morning. After taking care of various administrative responsibilities, I opened up the cougar website and my Yahoo instant messenger, and the games began! My "cubs," as I began calling them, were very attentive and eager, so the messages flooded in as soon as I signed on.

After half an hour of emotional and sexual stimulation from viewing sexy morning pics of a boy or two—a morning hello, if you will—I found I was absolutely ready to start the sexual energy transmutation with my wellness clients. The challenge came from being in a heightened physical and sexual "zone" while simultaneously making certain I could think and react mindfully in conversation with my clients. It took discipline and awareness to be so focused on work and to simultaneously maintain my playfulness and sexual energy. With practice, though, I learned how to flip the switch and transform my high emotional energy into enthusiasm, passion, and excitement for my work.

In communicating with my "boy toys," I soon found out that there is a standard sequential system to the dating process—a script, if you will. First, you connect on the cougar website. If that goes well, you proceed to personal email. Once you get to the email stage, that's usually when the guy will offer a picture of himself (which I always accepted). Then it moves on to instant messaging, which is my favorite part. In the IM stage, the guys start turning on their webcams! Technology is a wonderful thing.

The first time Mark asked me if I wanted to see him on cam, I said, "Sure, why not?" Little did I know that he would be naked, in a bathroom, masturbating! I really couldn't believe it…but I didn't shut him down either. There he was, standing bare-ass naked in what looked like a small office bathroom. He had the computer cam positioned so that I could only see him from the neck down. He was going at it with one hand and typing naughty messages to me with the other. Talented, I thought. Just before he was ready to cum, Mark reached for tissue paper that was perfectly folded, like a gentleman's handkerchief, to catch every drop. In the moment, I was more amused by this small act of fussy professionalism than I was by watching him jerk off. He didn't seem to mind that he couldn't watch me on camera, as long as I watched him. That fascinated me.

After a few weeks, I found myself comfortable with being sexually stimulated every day through sexting, viewing younger men masturbating in front of webcams, and becoming visually aroused by photographs. I'd go through my daily routine, working with my clients, marketing, promoting, and creating, but all the while, I'd be intentionally maintaining the strong flow of sexual energy. Most importantly, when I saw and experienced the positive influence my energy seemed to be having on my clients, the uneasiness and guilt I felt began to slowly fade away.

Soon, I found I was able to bring myself up into an almost euphoric state even without stimulation from the men on the website. Through self-awareness, however, I began to understand that *easy does it*. It didn't serve my purpose to operate under such constant and extreme levels of sexual energy; that was sure to cause quick burnout.

Over the course of about eight weeks, through trial and error, I figured out what worked best for me. Instead of looking for dramatic highs followed by depressing lows, I worked out a practice that incorporated a steady stream of energy throughout the day. I didn't allow myself to get over-stimulated to the point that I desired an orgasm (a sexual practice known as "edging," which can be quite exhausting, especially when entering and exiting the zone multiple times). I also didn't want a fast drop that could make me lose my vitality and enthusiasm, like a performer who spends all their energy on stage then crashes from sheer emotional exhaustion.

I experimented with a flirty, fun approach—I sent one energizing morning text or looked at a few sexy photos. The thought of naughtiness alone was enough to stimulate me. Once I found my energy balance, I felt great, confident, inspired, and enthusiastic. I was sleeping better than ever, and life was suddenly a lot more fun! It seemed impossible to be in a bad mood under this influence. I felt as if I'd really discovered something life-changing...

...until my new client, Helen, showed up in my life.

Chapter Three

TANTRIC SEX

—∞∞—

"Put away your pointless taboos and restrictions on sexual energy—rather help others to truly understand its wonder, and to channel it properly."

~GOD, CHANNELED BY NEALE DONALD WALSCH

When Helen arrived for her appointment, I felt an immediate connection. I loved talking to her! She was into yoga and many other activities that I loved learning about. I was itching to tell someone about my new discoveries, so I decided to take a risk and confide in her. She listened quietly as I told her my story of transformation, self-awareness, and sexual energy. She watched with interest as I showed her the cougar website where I'd been doing all my energy exchanges. Once I finished my story, Helen looked at me and said, "You know, that's Tantric sex."

"What's Tantric sex?" I asked her.

ENGAGING WITH THE
SPIRIT OF TANTRA

~

Okay, so I didn't uncover anything new. Instead, I was unknowingly practicing the 5,000-year-old ancient tradition of Tantric sex. The next question I had was, *If Tantric sex has been around for 5,000 years, why haven't I heard of it before now?* I was especially baffled by my ignorance when I found out that Tantra is at the heart of yoga, which I had been practicing for 13 years!

With a little research and guidance from Helen, I soon discovered that Tantra supports our natural desire to respect and cherish our bodies, minds, and spirits lovingly, holistically, healthfully, and expressively. The spiritual practice of Tantric sex is not only a physical practice, but also involves an emotional and energetic connection to our partner(s). I didn't have to be having physical sex with my "boy toys" to be practicing Tantric sex—we were practicing it just by communicating and creating sexual energy between us.

I quickly began to understand that the first thing I would need to do in order to openly explore the powerful possibilities of Tantric sex was to "look within" at my own shame, guilt, and limited perspectives on my sexuality and that of others. I needed to become less judgmental and more curious about sexual preferences, fantasies, and desires.

Before I knew it, another client presented me with the perfect opportunity to do just that. At the time, however, it was a path I had no intention or desire to travel down.

You Hear Rumors About These Things...

David scheduled a series of colonics with me, which meant he would be coming in once a week for six weeks to complete a full-body detoxification. Or so I thought. About 15 minutes into David's first procedure, he asked me, "Do you want to hear a crazy story about my cousin?" I was a little surprised. "Sure."

"My cousin and her girlfriends," David said, "love to dominate men. They took this guy to a secluded hallway at their local mall and made him get naked and bend over on his knees. Then one by one they stuck their high-heeled stilettos up his ass! Isn't that just too funny?"

My jaw dropped. I was completely shocked. Somehow I mustered a response. "Why on earth would anyone want to treat someone that way? And why would he let them? That's horrifying!" But David just chuckled and assured me, "He loved it. There are plenty of guys out there who want to be publicly humiliated and overpowered by a woman."

After David left my studio, I blew the whole experience off. *The guy was just a sick pervert who liked talking about sick shit,* I told myself. I didn't like it, but since I didn't feel like he posed any actual risk to me, I chose to continue with his detox program.

In later sessions, he was very honest and trusting with me. He even opened up about how he loves the freedom of being naked.

"Sandra, have you ever been to Sandy Hook beach?" I looked at him with eyebrows raised. I knew exactly where he was going with this conversation.

"No, I have never been to Sandy Hook. I have no desire to go to a nude beach. The last thing I want to see is some guy bending over and reaching for a beach ball as I'm having a chicken salad sandwich!"

David laughed, "Come on, it's a great feeling! It's so freeing to feel the breeze and sun on the body without clothes. I'll take you one day. You'll love it."

This guy was out of his mind if he thought I was going to get naked with him at some nude beach, but I didn't want him to think I judged him for enjoying it.

"Listen, if you like being naked in public, more power to you. Go for it!"

"Okay, so since you know I love being naked and you're comfortable with knowing that, would you mind if I do my treatments naked?"

I thought about it for a few minutes and replied, "Sure, get naked, but cover yourself with a towel."

In the weeks that followed, however, during his now-nude detox procedures with me, David regaled me with a litany of outrageous stories about his cousin and her freaky friends. More than a few of his stories still stand out in my mind:

- They took a guy into the woods, tied him to a tree for hours, and made him ejaculate in a glass over and over again. Once the glass was full, they made him drink it.
- They planned a dinner party where a particular "slave" cooked and served them food and cocktails. After the meal, the ladies made him perform oral sex on all of them (one by one) in front of the others.
- They picked up a guy at their local "club" to play with. Once they got him home they discovered he'd had his penis surgically removed at the demand of his former "Mistress." They nick-named him "Dickless."
- On one occasion, David's cousin took three guys, stripped them, had them face each other in a circle, and then tied their cocks together with rubber bands. She then played with their cocks until they all "came" all over each other.
- At one of the ladies' bridal shower, they had a guy fuck a blowup doll in front of all the guests.

I found these stories extremely disturbing, but I also found them a bit titillating. They were certainly piquing my already stimulated curiosity about sexual fantasies and desires, but it was difficult not to feel critical of the element of intense humiliation in each of the stories. I couldn't imagine myself ever speaking to anyone like that, let alone degrading them publicly or privately. *I am a caring, loving person,* I assured myself. *Studying the loving, compassionate, and healing practices of Tantric sex and playing with my "boy toys" certainly had nothing to do with these deranged idiots!*

The next week, I met privately with my yoga practitioner. I told her about how I had been transferring my sexual energy into my business, about playing with "my boys," and that I had been researching Tantra. After listening to my descriptions, she agreed with Helen's assessment that I had, in fact, been practicing Tantric sex. She then advised, "If you're interested in pursuing more knowledge on this ancient practice, I know of a reputable Tantra institute where I study," and handed me a brochure.

I wanted to get started right away. I had no real idea what I was getting myself into, and the tuition seemed steep for an online program, but I wanted to continue exploring my sexuality and making more of the new discoveries that had made my life so much better and more interesting lately.

The foundation of the program was a series of lectures, ritual ceremonies, breathing exercises, and yoga videos accompanied by reading material. It also encouraged students to travel to the institute in person to "experience enlightenment firsthand." I began the video lessons, and they were intriguing, despite the teacher's less-than-engaging style. He spoke slowly and quietly, and his snail's pace made me fidgety despite my interest in the ancient topic. I couldn't imagine going to the institute in person, listening to this slow-talker while sitting crossed-legged in a room full of hippies and gurus. My patience was running thin, but I was determined to keep studying.

EMBRACING THE WHOLE SELF

~✥~

A fter a few short weeks, I felt for the first time in my life as if what I really desired was possible. The best part was, I discovered through Tantra teachings that my dreams and desires didn't have to come at the expense of my health and well-being. In addition to self-empowerment, Tantra teaches that we are all connected through an invisible web, the omnipresence of the Universe, and that we attract back to ourselves the qualities that we already possess and express. In order to change my world, therefore, I needed to change my thoughts: to pursue the positive qualities of love, passion, forgiveness, hope, acceptance, purpose, joy, happiness, giving, receiving, kindness, and gratitude in order to attract the same qualities back to my life.

The key for me was to learn how to accept having "undesirable" feelings and to forgive myself (or others) for theirs. This was a hard lesson to learn and it certainly wasn't easy to practice at first. In fact, I often felt uncomfortable facing the real me. But over time I got better and better at it. Today, I am amazing at it.

Growing up, I was taught to be nice, smile, and to wear clear finger-nail polish. Now, when I feel like it, I'm stern, unsmiling, and wear red polish on my toes and fingernails.

Being Mistress Vivian has taught me that I don't always have to be nice—I can speak my mind and maintain strict boundaries with the people, places and things around me. I am no longer a dumping ground for other people's problems and expectations.

I vividly remember one session I had with a regular client. After I had him restrained, he told me, "Mistress, I love being with you. You make me feel alive. I no longer have a good relationship with my wife, and it's so stressful." Back in the day, I would have been open to letting him vent his stress out. I would have given him space to talk through his personal problems, even if it was at the expense of my own needs and desires. These days, no way! As soon as he finished his testimony, I threw only defiance back at him. "Do I look like your fucking girlfriend?" I asked sharply. "I'm not your fucking girlfriend!" (I slapped him in the face.) "I don't give a fuck what your problems at are at home!" (I spit in his face.) "You're here to amuse ME with your submission—I'm not here to listen to your shit!" (I kneed him in the stomach.) Real quick, he understood the rules of the relationship, and we proceeded to the ass-kicking segment of the session.

In my world outside of sessions, I don't need to slap, spit on, or kick someone to let them know I won't tolerate them dumping on me. I simply change the tone of the conversation, and if that doesn't work, I'm very straightforward in telling them to back off.

Often, people are offended when I call them out on something, but I don't soften the blow by saying nice things I don't mean. In other cases, though, I am amazed by how much others will respect my boundaries when I ask them to, allowing us to move on into a healthier relationship. Although it took me many years to gain the confidence necessary to be so assertive, the foundation for this personal growth came from my early practices in Tantra.

LEARNING TO SLOW DOWN

⤚⤛

After those first few sessions, I was hooked on Tantra. As my mind opened and my understanding deepened, my commitment to the practice intensified. I was willing to try anything...even things I already knew I didn't enjoy, like slowing down long enough to meditate.

When my yoga instructor suggested I meditate every day to complement my Tantra study, I thought, No way. I thought it was a waste of time. I appreciated the breathing exercises before, during, and after a yoga practice, but I couldn't imagine why the hell I needed to continue the practice on my own time. I had more important things to do. Besides, I was into Tantra for the sex! The bliss! The exciting energy! *Why slow down? How could that help me?*

When my progress stalled, however, I realized that if I wanted a true understanding of the practice of Tantra, I'd have to do some things that felt more like work, and less like play. I could either trust my teacher—who was far more knowledgeable about Tantra than I was—or do things that way I had always done. Determined to learn, I set aside my stubbornness and started meditating daily.

Tantra meditation practice uses prayer, asana (yoga postures), *mantra* (repetition of a phrase, such as *I am love, I am worthy, I am peaceful, I am safe,* and so on) and *pranayama* (control of the breath). When I practiced, I would sit in a comfortable position, close my eyes and do whatever came naturally to me. I didn't plan or try to control my meditation practice; I got out of the way and allowed it to evolve organically without any preconceived notions. This frequently involved praying to God, quieting my mind, and focusing on my breath. Through my concurrent studies and lectures, I also learned that one of the benefits of all these rituals is to awaken the sleeping energy inside, called *Kundalini Shakti,* or the raw spiritual Divine current. The most effective way to awaken this current is through the silencing of thoughts, energy, and emotion.

The chakras have a kind of spinning energy that comes from two basic currents, one from above and one from below. The *Kundalini* (coiled life force energy) lays dormant at the base of the spine until the *Shakti* (the Divine feminine energy) awakens it and carries the energy upward towards the crown where it meets the masculine Divine energy of Shiva. It is this interplay of masculine and feminine energy, the dual nature of our very existence, that is so transformative.

I was about to be introduced to the dual nature of sex in a very different way.

AN UNEXPECTED ENCOUNTER
WITH FETISHISM

I was first introduced to the fetish world by a 30-year-old, blonde haired, blue eyed personal trainer named Mitchell that I met on the cougar website. We weren't in an exclusive relationship, but once we trusted each other, he felt confident in disclosing his secret desires. From the beginning of our relationship, I'd felt that there was a unique sexual quality about Mitchell. This was intriguing to me, and sure enough, the first time we had sex together it became crystal clear that Mitchell not only enjoyed having sex with a woman, but he also had "pussy worship." There's really no other way to describe it. He wasn't trying to craft the sexual experience around his needs or impress me with his skills and talent—it was all about his desire to please me. I now understand he had a desire to be submissive, and in fact, "pussy worship" is a leading fetish in the BDSM community.

One weekend I texted Mitchell out of the blue. "You wanna play?" I asked. His immediate "YES" assured me he did. But when he added, "Do you get into D and S?" I was stumped. I had no idea what "D and S" was at the time. I asked him to explain.

"Domination and submission," texted Mitchell. "I'll do anything that pleases you, from cleaning your apartment to bathing you, or cooking and serving for you. In addition, I'll be your sex slave, and you can punish me by any means you see fit if I don't obey you."

Did I die and go to Heaven? This is too good to be true—or is it?

"Are you fucking with me?" I wrote. "Because I can totally get into this."

"Fucking with you? No," said the reply on my screen. "I have been looking for this type of relationship for a long time."

THERE'S LESS SEX THAN YOU MIGHT THINK

hhhhh...I get it. When I began studying Tantric sex, I thought it was all about having sex, but I soon learned that Tantric sex isn't some stand-alone sexual practice—it is based in the heart of the Tantra living philosophy. First, I do the loving work within myself, and only then am I able to begin applying the Tantra way of life to my sexual experiences with myself and others in order to create love, compassion, peace, happiness, health, wealth, and connection to the Divine. Anything can be Tantric. We could create a "Tantric Car Wash" as long as it was based in the loving Tantra living practices.

Tantra became my way of life. Once I silenced my critical and judgmental voices, curiosity took hold. I observed and noticed, rather than judged. My meditation practice led me into clarity. I focused on being grounded, fulfilling my desires, letting go of my ego and self-created fears. I practiced receiving and giving love and compassion. I spoke my mind. I trusted myself, God, and the

Universe, and expected miracles.

Tantric sex means truly embracing, honoring, and allowing ourselves and our partner(s) to be exactly who we are at any moment, whether it's through communication, energy exchange, or physical sex. In either case the decision to trust must come first. The less judgmental we are, the more intimate we become with our partner(s), and it's during our most intimate times that we discover more about ourselves as individuals.

THE BIGGER THE RISK, THE BIGGER THE PAYOFF

O ne afternoon while chatting with my "cub" Trevor online, I found myself once again discovering something new about myself. Trevor and I had not met in real life; we inspired each other's creativity and endeavors only through online chats. We felt a strong positive connection with one another. One day Trevor suggested that I ask my lover, Jay (who I also met on the cougar dating website), if he would be comfortable having Trevor listen in on the phone while Jay and I were having sex. Jay and I had been seeing each other for almost a year and were exclusive lovers.

"I don't know if he'll go for it," I said, "but I'll ask." I texted Jay, "Hey, I have an online guy friend who wants to listen in while we're having sex. Just so you know, I have never had sex with him, or even met him." After about a minute or so, a text came back from Jay: "Great, how about tonight?" Well, I'll be damned! I hadn't expected him to agree so easily. We set it up for around 11:00 p.m. When Jay arrived at my apartment, he found me in sexy lingerie and high heels, with a bottle of red wine in my hand.

After a few passionate kisses hello, I called Trevor to begin our threesome. Jay got into it right away, but I needed a little coaching. After a while Jay looked up at me. "Don't be shy," he said. "It's fine."

I relaxed and went with the flow. Soon I forgot about the phone altogether. I was entirely focused on being with my lover. After about an hour of play, Jay reached over and turned off the phone. "Now it's just you and me, baby," he said. That's when the party really got started. After he hung up the phone with Trevor, the sex between us was tremendous. We had taken a risk together, which created a closer bond between us and lifted our emotional, physical, and spiritual sexual connection up into the stratosphere!

Before this experience I would have jumped straight into fearfully thinking, *He must not love me or respect me if he's willing to share me with someone else,* but I replaced those old negative thoughts with new, more loving ones, like, *He must really love and trust me enough to explore our intimate sexuality together.*

Along with the mental and spiritual healing aspects of this loving practice, there is also the huge physical healing component in Tantra. And, believe it or not, orgasm is not the primary intention in Tantric sex. I know, I know. The thought of not reaching an orgasm was hard for me to accept at first too, but once I began to understand the importance of being present with my partner, exchanging energy and enjoying the freedom of expression, sex became so much more than physical pleasure, and a lot more blissful too—not to mention the increased vitality, mental focus, and energy levels. It is worth adding that, once achieved, the orgasmic experience through this practice may be prolonged (up to 20 minutes), offering stronger and more frequent orgasms because the body sends the energy up through the *Kundalini Shakti*.

ADAPTING THE SEXUAL CEREMONY

Tantric sex focuses on the benefits of prolonging the sexual experience, or "ceremony," for increased intimacy and sometimes for better health. In ancient times, partners spent hours or days within this sexual ceremony, however, in our fast-paced modern lives, this could prove to be challenging—and that's where technology can step in! The ceremony could begin with a transfer of sexual energy through sexting or sending sexy photos, and then become physical later that day, or even that week. Once physical elements have been introduced, rituals may include body massage, watching or looking at erotica, bathing, role-playing, feeding one another, undressing and admiring each other's physical body, prolonged eye contact, making out, dancing, changing sexual positions, and sensation play (feathers, ice, biting, spanking). Use your imagination and all five senses. Take your time. Be in the moment—forget the past, let the future be a mystery, and choose a time and place to be thoughtful and intentional about your sexual experience.

This is not to say there's anything wrong with a "quickie," but the more time we spend cultivating our sexual energy, the stronger its influence becomes on the chemistry of the brain. Positive sexual experiences prompt the endocrine glands to release healthy hormones and chemicals, such as:

- HGH: A natural growth hormone produced by the pituitary gland that helps maintain the health of tissues and organs, in addition to reducing fat in the body, smoothing the skin, and increasing vitality, energy, and resilience. HGH is sometimes referred to as the "Fountain of Youth."
- SEROTONIN: The "happy" neurotransmitter is found primarily in the "gut," the pineal gland, blood platelets, and the nervous system. Serotonin helps regulate mood, feelings associated with wellbeing, sexuality, and appetite. It is also a natural sleep aid.
- DHEA: This hormone functions as the precursor in the development of sexual hormones, estrogen in women and testosterone in men. DHEA is produced in the adrenal glands.
- OXYTOCIN: Termed the "cuddle hormone," oxytocin is produced naturally in the hypothalamus in the brain. Oxytocin may be conditioned to release after a pattern of sex with the same lover has been established. Just seeing your lover can release more oxytocin, making you want to be with that person all the more.

This is what we think of as a "chemical attraction" or "having chemistry" with another person.

Tantric sex also increases blood circulation, which improves overall sexual health. The concomitant (or simultaneous) deep breathing helps detoxify the body, and the increased heart rate means a strengthened immune system. All of these factors contribute to rejuvenation and longevity.

TANTRA FOR ALL LIFE STAGES

T he more I practiced the lifestyle of Tantra, the more I could see emotional and physical health benefits within myself. I was happy, energized, and sleeping restfully. Most impressively, I am now experiencing menopause without any emotional or physical symptoms!

When I turned 50, I started to wonder when I would start menopause and how my body and mind would respond. In January 2009, I skipped my first period at the age of 52, and the hot flashes quickly followed. I wasn't even sure at the time that they were hot flashes because I just felt a warm rush run though my body every so often. I thought to myself, *Fine, if this is the extent of my menopausal symptoms, I can definitely handle it.* Even though I was coping well, I was still grateful to stumble upon a remedy for all my menopausal symptoms: Tantric sex!

Decreased serotonin alone may cause menopausal symptoms such as depression, anxiety, carbohydrate cravings, hot flashes, insomnia, and mood swings. Five years after my first hot flash, I am not experiencing any menopausal symptoms. No mood swings, nothing. Sexually, I am functioning better than I did in my younger years. My neurotransmitters and sexual hormones are performing perfectly, my libido is strong, I have increased sexy confidence, no vaginal dryness, and no monthly period. It doesn't get any better than this! A good healthy sex drive is a sign of good heath and shows that the body is in balance.

I'm so convinced that we are not as simple as some of us would like to believe, and that our physical and "logical" realities barely scratch the surface of who we are. We all have an amazing ability to not only heal ourselves emotionally and physically, but we also contain a spiritual energy that enables us to manifest love, happiness, depth, and compassion. I believe we are so much more than purely physical beings—I believe we are connected deeply to everything *and everyone* through the vibrational omnipresence of the Universe, and I believe that through this connection, we can directly influence our physical reality and personal happiness.

THE SWITCH

*"Begin to see yourself as a soul with a body rather
than a body with a soul."*

~WAYNE W. DYER

Chapter Four

ONENESS

———⚬⚬⚬———

"A person experiences life as something separated from the rest—a kind of optical delusion of consciousness. Our task must be to free ourselves from this self-imposed prison, and through compassion, to find the reality of Oneness."

~ALBERT EINSTEIN

Along with my organic discovery of the power of sexual energy, the Tantra teachings of energy and emotional self-awareness, and my studies into the realm of "Oneness" through metaphysical science, I began to study transmutation of emotion and energy. It turns out that not only will the Universe fulfill our needs and desires; the Universe gives us everything we need and desire in the fastest and easiest way possible, including the people we meet along the way to help and support us through our journey.

I have always taken more of a scientific approach to thinking and making decisions. In my professional studies, I focused on subjects like exercise physiology, holistic nutrition, and aromatherapy. I find the miracles of the human body fascinating. I am left-brain dominant, and have always favored rational, strategic, logical thought, as well as "being in control." This explains why it took a while to for me to come around to the Tantra philosophy.

As fate would have it, I met a woman who would help me understand the universal connection between science and spirit. Nancy made an appointment at my wellness center to address her serious digestive issues. After only four visits, we started to trust and confide in one other. Although Nancy is extremely beautiful, successful, and very happily married, she confessed that her sex life was lacking, but she qualified this by saying she accepted it. I listened to her story with sympathy, and wondered to myself if she would be open to exploring her sexuality through Tantra.

Some time later during one of her treatments, I finally found the courage to ask her. "Have you ever heard of Tantric sex?" She said no, and looked at me with puzzled curiosity as I carefully described this ancient, loving, spiritual practice of self-awareness, and the philosophy behind creating intimacy and trust with a partner.

Nancy quickly rejected the notion of exploring the practice, claiming her relationship with her husband was a loving "companionship and friendship," and that she was not interested in rocking the "happy family" boat. I tried to make her feel more at ease, and to pique her curiosity by disclosing that for a while I'd been studying and successfully practicing how to transfer my sexual energy into my business for the manifestation of prosperity and abundance.

"Have you ever heard of *The Secret?*" she asked me.

The Secret is a documentary-style film produced by Ronda Byrne in 2006. It incorporates interviews with modern day practitioners of the Law of Attraction and ancient theories on how we can use our emotions and positive energy to manifest abundance in all areas of our lives. My experience with ancient Tantra studies for sexual energy transmutation and manifestation allowed me to instantly relate to the concept of the film. Soon, I began exploring what such information could mean to me personally, and—if it were really true that we were all "connected" in such a deep yet unseen way—how it would change my life. The first thing I realized was that I could no longer believe in "accidents" or "coincidences" the way I used to. I had a very clear understanding at that moment that this was a turning point in my life, and that my life would never be the same.

FEELINGS ARE THERE
FOR A REASON

W hen Jay and I met we had an instant connection with one another, and not just in the sense of physical attraction. On countless occasions one of us would contact the other when a "feeling" hit us. I tried to explain it to my friend Serena one evening, but found it difficult.

"It's not like I'm trying to send him "signals" or "conjure" him up. He can feel when I'm thinking about him or feeling strong emotions that include him."

"Does it happen when you're happy to be thinking about him?"

I thought for a minute. "Sometimes, but he can also sense when my thoughts aren't so pleasant, like after a conflict. The Universe doesn't seem to be partial about whether feelings are good or bad," I explained. "It just arranges and directs accordingly. So, Jay gets the signal—one way or the other."

I told her about a recent text he had sent me: "If you don't want to see me anymore, quit sending me that energy!" I told him how much it freaked me out when that kind of thing happened, and he agreed, as did Serena.

It's not easy to be aware of all our feelings. It can be even harder to connect with them, especially if they make us uncomfortable. I never considered myself a feeler. I wasn't brought up in a family where I could express my emotions freely. Instead, I was taught that my worth came from "how much I could take" *without* indulging in feelings.

Needless to say, it was unsettling to experience this level of connectedness with another person. Jay could sense when I was upset, lonely, or in need of emotional support—all things that I would rarely express to him on my own, let alone ask for help with. It was strange, too, to realize how influenced I could be by Jay's emotional state and the signals he was sending me whether he meant to or not.

WHAT DO YOU REALLY WANT?

❧

A ll of our thoughts and feelings vibrate on different levels, and these vibrations travel out into the Universe to bring us new circumstances, which resonate with those energetic pulses. Every day, the vibrations of our thoughts and feelings shape our physical reality. Our internal conversations and those we have with others are superb indicators of the kinds of vibrational energies we're projecting to the world. Similar energies attract, meaning that the messages you send yourself, the environment you create, and the people you surround yourself with all impact the state of your reality.

The same principle applies to our asking the Universe for our desires and dreams. Once we ask, receive, and take action, the next steps will be unfolded before us, which will lead us to our desired results.

COPING WITH CHANGING DESIRES

❧

J ay and I had been dating for two years when I decided I was no longer interested in continuing the relationship the way it was going. And I told him so. It wasn't an ultimatum; it was more of a turning point.

"I am willing to work at our relationship," I explained, "but you need to give me something to work with. I can no longer settle for a relationship where we only spend time together two to three times a month."

When Jay and I had met, I was working 12 to 14 hours a day, seven days a week, leaving me very little energy to invest in a real, full-time relationship. Jay also had—and still has—a very demanding job (about which he expressed loathing every time I saw him), that kept his schedule turning on a dime.

On many occasions he texted or called me at the last minute to cancel our plans. In the past, this quasi-relationship worked for me. Quite frankly, I always felt that Jay was doing me a favor by canceling because I was usually way too tired to give a shit and was glad of the chance to go straight home from work, drink two glasses of wine, and then go to sleep. That way I could get some rest, get up the next morning, and do it all over again.

So, for a while, our schedules were equally busy, and our lives aligned…but then I became free and he was still doing time.

The relationship no longer fit the direction that I was pursuing, and I realized that by continuing to stay with Jay I would be keeping myself on my old path. As wonderful as he was, his energy was no longer right for me and the strength of our connection was weakening as his negative energy slowly changed mine.

I had been telling the Universe that I wanted change and the time had come for me to prove it.

TIME TO LEAP

⌒

O nce I understood and believed this law of the Universe that "like energy attracts like energy," it was time for me to have fun creating a life I loved. I was curious, and even a little doubtful, about how this mysterious omnipresence would deliver me all my hopes and dreams, but the more I learned about the philosophy and substantiation behind this spiritual and scientific truth, the more my doubts faded.

My perception of the Law of Attraction was that I could have anything I wanted, and that the Universe had no concept of big or small. All I needed to do was believe that once I asked, my desires and dreams would be delivered to me in one form or another. The next question was, what did I really want? I had to step back and really do some soul searching about my true desires. I didn't see the point in holding back either. I thought to myself, *Why not go for it? The bigger the better!* and I started on my wish list.

It was time to focus on what I wanted—for me, personally. And, what I really wanted was to have a real life. I looked around me. Life had been passing me by and I was no longer content to let that to happen. I wanted to be surrounded by nature, and to be healthy and peaceful. I wanted to walk outside in the morning at a beach home on the ocean to watch the sunrise with my lover, friends, and family. I wanted to live in Manhattan in an amazing apartment with a killer view, so that anytime I wanted to explore the most amazing city in the world, all I'd need to do was take the elevator down to the lobby floor and go. I wanted to be in a loving, trusting, happy, fun, passionate relationship with a hot, interesting, sexy, affectionate guy. I wanted to spend quality time with friends and family. I wanted to serve and be creative and expand into the most amazing unimaginable projects for the good of all. *I wanted a fucking life!*

Like most folks, I could not fathom that I could personally be so powerful that I had it within me to change the arrangement of the Universe through visualizing and setting my intentions. That seemed like some crazy shit! But now I know it is the truth, and it can be true for everyone. We are all created in God's image equally. Not one of us has been sprinkled with an extra dash of pixie dust.

Despite my reservations, I put every thought and feeling I had toward my intentions. There was no holding back. Every action, every meditation, every visualization, every prayer, every tear of gratitude, every faithful moment, every moment of receiving, every moment of giving, and every powerful affirmation I had reaffirmed my guiding statement:

I am unconditional love, I am compassionate, I am giving.
I am safe, I am secure, I am nature.
I am grateful, I am happy, I am healthy, I am joyful.
I am successful, I am wealthy.
I am in love, I am inspired, I am worthy.
I AM WHOLE.

Every breath, fiber, and cell in my body, mind, and soul was 100 percent joined in the goal of manifesting and creating the life of my dreams.

Only, I had no idea that I was going to have to let go of everything I had and everything I thought I knew in order to make that dream into a reality. It was as if God was saying, "I want to give you all of this, but if you want everything you're asking for, you need to make space, and that means getting rid of things..."

And so it was that everything in my life crashed and burned.

Chapter Five

THE BLESSING IN DISGUISE

———⚬⚬⚬———

"It's okay to be crazy and scared and brave at the same time!"

~KELLY EPPERSON

I have always had a dominant personality. I'm not a bitch, *per se*, but I have a well defined "do no harm, but take no shit" attitude—it has served me well as a dominatrix. I will stand up for myself even when I'm afraid to do so. Defending your *true self* from the things you fear, or worse, from the things you love can be terrifying, but there are times in life when we have to be warriors.

THINGS FALL APART

———⚬———

It was beautiful Friday afternoon. I was in a great mood. My co-worker and I were in the middle of a good laugh when the front door opened and a man entered.

"Sandra LaMorgese?"

"That's me," I said.

"I need you to sign here."

It was a letter from a client's attorney.

My heart pounded as I slid the paper out of the envelope and unfolded it. Fear rushed through me. I closed my eyes for a minute to do some deep breathing exercises, gathering my composure.

"What's wrong?" asked my coworker. "What is that?"

I looked at her. "This is serious," I said, and managed to make it back to my chair before I collapsed.

My friend Tami had recently brought her boyfriend Tyson in for a colonic. He and I had a phone consultation and a face-to-face discussion about his personal information, medical history, overall health, and other symptoms to determine whether the procedure was appropriate. This was a step I always took very seriously in my practice, and if anything sounded questionable we would not move forward—but there was nothing in Tyson's history that would preclude him from colon hydrotherapy, so I determined that we could proceed with the appointment. The procedure went well and Tyson felt great. He even scheduled a series of future appointments for himself. Then, later that evening, I got a call from the hospital.

"My patient had no business inserting a speculum in his rectal area after the radical surgery he underwent," Tyson's physician told me.

"Excuse me?" I was shocked. "What are you talking about? This is the first time I'm hearing anything about this."

Now the doctor sounded surprised. I heard him say to Tyson, "You mean to tell me that you never told this woman you had rectal surgery?"

I was completely stunned. Prior conditions and contraindications were the focus of our in-person consultation. Had Tyson disclosed this surgery to me, the colonic would never have happened. Fortunately, he was going to be okay. I was shaken up, of course, but relieved that there would be no permanent damage and that the business I'd spent a decade of my life building was not ruined by the incident. Then the summons came.

I was being sued for neglect.

When the man arrived at my wellness studio with the legal papers, I was totally devastated. I couldn't believe it. I read through the papers, shaking and scared. There was no way I was going to take this sitting down. I couldn't afford an attorney because I'd just invested all my savings into renovations for the studio. This meant I was going to see this thing out by going to court and presenting my case on my own. To my horror, though, the suit grew to include the manufacturer of the of hydrotherapy equipment, the medical professional who wrote prescriptions for the colon hydrotherapy supplies, and, it seemed to me, anyone they could think of to accuse. It was one thing to deal with a possible personal financial judgment against me, but I couldn't stand by while other healthcare professionals were punished unjustly.

Over the next month or so I kept in mind everything I'd learned about meditation, observation, and consciousness. In my old way of thinking and feeling, I would have jumped to conclusions and made immediate and impulsive changes, but this time I didn't move so fast. I waited for Divine intervention. Yes, I was scared, but I felt confident and hopeful at the same time. I was beginning to realize that up until that point, following my instincts and applying the Law of Attraction to my life had been almost easy compared to this. Using my sexual energy to attract new partners or new business was fun. Now, though, I was in the midst of a stressful and fast-paced situation, and it became much more difficult to sit back, calm my mind, and allow signs and opportunities to appear. I felt almost cheated by the sudden turn of events. When I originally decided to trust God, myself, and the Universe, I didn't count on this devastating circumstance! I was in it for the bliss, happiness, love, and abundance! Not the bad stuff! With the summons looming on my desk, the last thing I wanted to do was meditate or trust.

But I did it anyway.

Although it sure didn't feel like a blessing at the time, I refused to worry about it or to feel bad about it. I had to take responsibility, but I did not have to become emotionally and physically sick over it. I had so many other things in my life to be grateful for, and I knew it was my choice to remain happy and hopeful.

A TEST OF FAITH

A few days later, I was folding spa towels in the relaxation room and thinking through my legal strategy when a voice whispered in my ear, "You don't always have to win."

Something about this little voice made me sit up and take notice. I trusted this voice implicitly, and the voice was telling me that I could let it all go. I was suddenly overwhelmed by the feeling that maybe, letting go was not a bad thing. Maybe it was the best thing for me. I needed to trust that, even though I didn't understand how, the Universe was lining up everything to fit perfectly with my hopes and dreams. I felt grateful for the new perspective, and after that realization, I felt thoroughly protected and safe.

My "award winning" wellness studio had been open for two years when I had to make one of the hardest decisions of my life. Yes, I had decided to trust God and the Universe, but having all the trust in the world won't keep you from being really, fucking scared sometimes. In a conversation with my naturopathic-mastermind friend Michael, I found the courage to say, "Michael, help me. I made the decision to close my wellness studio. I am scared."

He looked at me. "Are you divorced?" he asked, as he motioned for me to stand up so that he could guide me through a series of "muscle testings" as I answered his questions.

I nodded.

"How did you feel afterwards?"

"Good," I said, not knowing where he was going with this.

"Look at closing your studio like another bad relationship, and then break it off. Your body and emotions are expressing that you'll be in a better place afterwards. You need to be free. You need to fly."

I knew Michael was right, but the idea of no income, no savings, and no prospects was terrifying. I was single and living alone, and had no family members to help me, which left me in the precarious position of having to trust in the Universe one hundred percent that my life would unfold the way I wanted it to.

I was at the point that most of us eventually reach, when it's time to make a change of great magnitude—when it's time to say, "Fuck it!" and let it fly.

Chapter Six

THE BIG BANG!

——∞∞∞——

*"Faith is the bird that feels the light and sings when
the dawn is still dark."*

~RABINDRANATH TAGORE

It was 1:30 p.m. on a Wednesday afternoon. I was already sitting in the chair across from the lawyer's desk when he arrived. He came into his office, sat down, and introduced himself. I looked him straight in the eye. "I'm in quite a pickle," I told him. He smiled and confirmed that, "most people sitting in that chair generally are," and asked me to explain. I proceeded to calmly tell him about my situation, and we spent a good 45 minutes reviewing my options.

"So," I asked, "How do I make this go away?"

He didn't hesitate: "File for bankruptcy."

Wow. That thought had never crossed my mind.

I've spent my entire life maintaining an excellent credit score and always paying back anyone who ever helped me out by lending me money. I've always felt a high sense of pride and responsibility in paying my bills on time and being a good provider for my son as a single mother. I was the workhorse, always with two jobs or running my own business.

During this time in my life, however, I found I had to abandon my ego and pride. I had to give up control of what I saw as my safety, security, and reputation and instead trust God and the Universe to provide my stability.

Things moved swiftly over the next couple of weeks, and, to my great relief and with due gratitude to the Universe, everything fell perfectly into place. After a couple of days and a single phone call, I negotiated a deal for the sale of all my wellness studio's devices, equipment, and furnishings. I only got a fraction of their worth, but I felt grateful for the help, and I tried to remember that these things had served me well during my career in wellness. Of course, as a stipulation of my negotiation with the lawyer, I insisted on a good faith payment up front so I could get the ball rolling with the legal proceedings. I needed cash. The deal on the equipment was my only option.

My accountant was incredibly helpful, working with me to get the financial papers completed even though he knew I didn't have the funds to pay him. All he asked was not to be included in the bankruptcy, which he wasn't. (It gives me enormous pleasure now each time I write him a check to pay off the remaining balance. Every time my pen touches the paper check, I feel my heart melting for what my friend did for me in my time of need.) The financial maneuvering was difficult, and the thought of walking away from the practice that I spent years building still broke my heart, but the most painful part of the process by far was breaking my responsibilities to my clients and saying goodbye.

Months earlier, I had confided in my client Jill that I was using sexual energy transmutation for the means of prosperity. Now I confided in her about my suffering as she was trying to comfort me during the final days of my studio. "I feel like everything is out of my hands. It's killing me to not fulfill my responsibility."

"Maybe this is a lesson for you to do your own personal work," she suggested compassionately.

I knew she was right, even though it didn't make me feel much better. What did help, however, was telling Jill the truth. I decided it might make me feel even better if I started disclosing to a few clients that I was closing the studio and walking away from the business. Every client I told about my plans kept asking me the same question: "What are you going to do for work?" Every time, I answered, "I don't know. I've just decided to move toward my joy, and let the Universe do its thing."

While I navigated my ongoing disappointment about my studio closing, I was thoroughly surprised by how well I was handling the so-called devastation in my life. I felt gratitude and amazement more than anything else. In fact, I felt secure in my belief that all was well in the Universe and that God had a plan for me. My faith had grown stronger than the lies and fears I had carried with me all my life. In the end, what seemed like the most catastrophic event I would ever experience turned out to be a blessing instead.

On December 10, 2011, I officially closed my wellness studio and packed up my personal belongings. The more I packed, disassembled, and folded up, the more I felt the energy in the space changing. My friend and coworker came by in the early evening to help me finish. "The energy is completely different in here!" she exclaimed.

"Yeah, and that energy is walking out the door," I agreed. "The energy is us."

At that moment, I realized that my only true attachment to the space came from my ego—for how impressive having my own studio and business made me look to the rest of the world. As I thought about my energy, however, I realized that I still had all my passion, education, and purpose within me. I wasn't losing anything truly meaningful— only the space that helped me learn to express myself—and that, I knew, was replaceable. Once the boxes were filled and carried down to the Jeep along with my books, framed degrees, awards, and client records, it was time to make one last return up to what I called the "Hall of Gratitude."

A JOURNEY OF GRATITUDE

The Hall of Gratitude began as two white poster boards on which my clients wrote down the things they were grateful for, at my encouragement. The boards were started in 2009 by an eight-year-old girl who was bored one afternoon while waiting for her mom, who was seeing me for a nutritional assessment. Usually, I posted my upcoming events and speaking engagements on the white board so that my clients could join in on the fun. But that day, instead of updating the event postings, I decided to offer the board to my client's daughter instead, so that she could draw while she waited.

The little girl's eyes lit up at the thought of doing something creative. She sweetly and quietly took a marker and the board over to a cozy black reception chair and began drawing. For the entire 30-minute appointment, we never heard a peep from her. When we'd finished the assessment, her mother and I walked over to see the work of art that the girl had been focused on so intently.

The first thing I noticed was a drawing of me as a rock star, adorned in a skimpy Britney Spears outfit and singing into a microphone. The girl had written "Sandra" underneath the drawing, so that everyone would know that it was me. I loved it—my hips had never looked smaller! But once I got past the ego trip, I looked into the upper left-hand corner and saw, written in an earnest, childish hand: "What are you grateful for?" and underneath, "Write it down." Her mother and I were in awe. Such a young girl with so much enlightenment! Her words were so precious that I felt compelled to share them. I re-hung the newly christened "Gratitude Board" in the spirit of love, and was the first person to write on it: "Forgiveness." Before long, my clients also began to record their gratitude where everyone could read it.

When two entire boards were full, we started writing on the walls.

Before I knew it, the walls of the hallway were filled with testimonies of gratitude. I even had a special sign made that read "The Hall of Gratitude" for the entrance, which clients could see as soon as they walked in the front door. Some of the statements were silly and fun, but mostly they thanked God for hope, health, prosperity, relationships, family, love, and good friends. These were very private thoughts and feelings and many of my clients needed privacy and a few minutes alone before they began writing. It was so emotional for some clients that they thought for weeks in advance before they wrote anything.

The night I was closing my doors for good, I slowly moved through the facility, taking pictures of all the testimonies in the Hall of Gratitude and feeling the love one more time with tears flowing down my face. I was so grateful for the work that I was able to do there and could only trust that I would find similar joy and fulfillment in the next chapter of my life.

That night, after closed the door for the final time, I sensed I would be on my own for weeks until I had the emotional strength to start reaching out to others. I did my best to stay in the positive flow of the Universe and keep my mind off pointless worrying. I outlined my reality:

I'm 55 years old.

I have a few bucks in the bank, no savings, and no partner or family to support me.

I have no job prospects.

I just filed for bankruptcy.

I have no credit cards and no worldly means of getting a loan.

And I was facing this alone.

For the most part I kept it together during the day by mediating, working out, reading every book by Eckert Tolle and Gregg Braden that I could get my hands on, or watching Wayne Dyer and Abraham videos that I found on YouTube until I was exhausted. Anything to keep me in the zone. But the evenings, when I was tired and alone, took a toll on me.

I sank into a very dark place, one I had never been in before and never want to see again. One filled with lost hope and feelings of worthlessness. Red wine and cigarettes were my best friends during that time—something I would have hated myself for only months before.

Then one night, before I went to bed, I had a chat with God. (I was talking, God was listening.) "God, I love You and trust You. I'm going to bed tonight and I'm asking You to help me out. Please, don't let me suffer anymore. Bring me home to You tonight. Or, when I wake up in the morning in peace, I'll keep moving towards my dreams." Things started turning around in the morning when I woke up still breathing and believing God had answered my prayer. I switched from the "woe is me" attitude to realizing that I had so much to be grateful for. *I am healthy, intelligent, and resourceful,* I told myself. *I am focused, confident, and hopeful. My son is safe; I am safe; my sister and her family are all well and healthy.* My gratitude list went on and on. I didn't have any urgent or life-threatening concerns, I realized. I just needed to generate income. I always feel excited, open-minded, and confident when I get an inspirational message, but even I raised my eyebrows at this sudden change in perspective.

AN UNLIKELY SOLUTION

"Is it illegal to be a dominatrix?"

I was sitting with my friend and wellness client Serena, who had just asked me the same old question about my income: "What are you going to do, Sandra?" But this time, as soon as she asked, an inspirational thought popped into my head, and those strange words came flowing unbidden out of my mouth.

I'm not sure where the idea came from. Perhaps it was all the sexual energy I was using to manifest. Maybe it came from my dominance experience with my cub, or from the stories about David's cousin and her girlfriends having fun with male slaves. I don't know. The thought seemed to just appear out of nowhere.

Serena looked at me. "I don't think so," she said. "After all, a dominatrix doesn't have sex."

My mind rejected the idea as fast as it had created it, and I laughed out loud. "NO! Get the fuck out of here!" I exclaimed, still chuckling. But Serena wasn't so quick with negativity and began to flirt with the idea out loud.

"Why couldn't you do it?" she asked. "You've been doing all this sexual empowerment work. It's a perfect 'walk the walk and talk the talk' on sexual energy transmutation, Tantric sex, and unbridled female sexuality."

"Really, you think so?" I asked, suddenly warming to the idea. I mean, what the hell? I had nothing to lose by trying. And I was willing to bet a good dominatrix could make some pretty good money!

But where could I apply for such a job? And how would I get the position even if I found an establishment practicing this sort of thing? Would they hire a woman over 50 with no experience whatsoever? I Googled "dominatrix jobs in New York City."

I found a blog on which a woman mentioned she'd completed one day of training as a dominatrix in New York City but decided never to return to The Dungeon due to its "extreme atmosphere of sadomasochism in forms of physiological humiliation and physical torture."

Hmm…

I called The Dungeon on the spot, and asked for an interview.

FINDING NIRVANA

"The secret of happiness is freedom, the secret of freedom is courage."

~Carrie Jones, Need

Chapter Seven

THE INTERVIEW

—⊗∞⊗—

"When one has nothing to lose, one becomes courageous. We are timid only when there is something we can still cling to."

~Don Juan

I f you want to work in New York City, you've got to have thick skin. If you don't, you might find yourself with your tail between your legs on the next bus to whatever small town you came from.

I suppose one of the reasons I could hold my ground with the "take no shit" Dungeon managers, dominant Mistresses, and high-powered Wall Street executive clients is because I had years of experience working in New York City with acting and modeling agents who could be particularly pretentious, quick to reject, and generally cold as ice. Just as I'd had to work hard to get the jaded and demanding agent's attention by sending my headshots, attending open calls, and auditioning, I needed to work even harder to get someone to notice me at a BDSM club.

The afternoon I called The Dungeon, all I heard on the other end was "Hello" in a noticeably unengaged tone. I didn't know who I needed to speak with, or even if I had the right number. I began with "Hi, I'm interested in setting up a job interview." The icy voice asked,

"Do you have pictures?" For a split second the question confused me. The last thing I wanted to do was appear uninformed about why The Voice had asked me for pictures, thereby endangering any hope I had of an interview. I recovered quickly, and lied: "Yes, yes I do."

After I confirmed I had pictures, The Voice told me to send them to the email address on the Dungeon's website. Then I heard a click. It took me a minute to realize that The Voice had hung up. That was it? No more information than that? Just "send pictures"?

Thinking back, it's no wonder it took them so long to give me the time of day. They must have had a good laugh when my acting head-shot arrived along with a photo of me in my bra and panties in a picture I took for one of my cubs. I figured they'd want to see my face and whether I had a nice figure. This made sense to me. How was I to know that they were expecting to see me decked out from head to toe in leather and latex in the middle of an elaborate BDSM dominatrix photo shoot?

Three days later when I hadn't heard from them, I sent a follow-up email thanking them for their consideration and requesting an in-person interview. Days later, there was still no response. All I could think of was how crazy this whole idea was, and that there was no way I was going to get hired in an NYC dungeon as a professional dominatrix! Why would they hire me? I had no experience. I wasn't 25 years old, and I was certainly no longer a size four.

That said, I figured I'd be broke within a month and possibly seeking shelter, and I knew that this was the way to get back on my feet financially. I wanted to do it even though I knew I was going to "ruin" my reputation by working in this taboo industry; even though I was sure my son and sister were going to turn their backs on me as well, I knew I had to take the risk. Serena had a very good point when she suggested that my working in this industry would clearly mean I was "walking the walk" by making choices that worked for me and not acting based on my fears.

Furthermore, how could I fully embrace Tantric sex, partner acceptance, power and energy exchange and so on, if I held on to judgment and fear? It all made sense, but I couldn't even imagine what it would be like to work in a BDSM Dungeon. It would have been less bizarre if I'd woken up one morning with the sudden urge to become an astronaut.

On The Dungeon's website, they state that under no condition is "sex" permitted in any shape or form. This more than eased my concerns. It actually made everything else seem like gravy. Other than the sheer absurdity of the idea in the first place, I kept having this intuitive, reassuring thought from the Universe that I desperately wanted to trust. I remembered that within the omnipresence of the Universe, all things are possible—even me becoming a professional dominatrix!

But no matter how hard I tried to talk myself into such a possibility, there was nothing in my reality telling me that it was possible. I alternated between excited hope and despair when my logical side kicked in. I was struggling with all the negative social influences that told me how wrong I would be to make such a decision. At the same time, I felt I needed to be true to myself and that the experience could empower me as a woman. I somehow understood that this would set me free from my own judgmental perceptions, social standards, and "rules" for how a woman should behave.

I became aware that all these thoughts were emotional roadblocks. I was standing in my own way by letting my fear trump my hope, allowing trepidation to win over persistence.

At that moment, I knew what I needed to do. I needed to keep sending emails to The Dungeon until they finally gave in and offered me an interview! I was not going to give up and let emotional roadblocks bring my life to a halt. My focus changed from what I didn't have to what I did have. *Yeah, sure, I'm not 25 and a size four, but I am a very attractive woman rocking dangerous curves. I don't have experience, but that never stopped me from pursuing anything.* I decided right then and there I was going to make this happen!

I sat down at my computer and said, "Fuck it," as I wrote another email to the mysterious Voice at The Dungeon.

Hello,

I am still interested in coming in to meet you personally to discuss my possibilities for employment. Do not let my Tantra Zen fool you. I am totally capable of handling the position. In addition, I'm not afraid of hard work and learning the ropes.

Thanks,

Sandra

Still no answer on the other end, but at this stage I was feeling better simply because I was taking action and not worrying about "what could happen." I refused to imagine going backward in my life. That was my old way of thinking! I was not sinking down or standing still—I was moving up!

WHAT DID WE DO BEFORE GOOGLE?

On Christmas Eve, I was getting ready to head out to dinner with a friend of mine who was celebrating his birthday. Thomas and I had met three years prior at my wellness studio. He had initially contacted me through a referral from one of my other clients, and we had always maintained a casually friendly relationship. Towards the final six months that my studio was open, however, we'd become closer and started spending time together socially.

I was really looking forward to dinner that evening. We had reservations at the steakhouse right down the road from my apartment. I'd eaten there numerous times, and always had a great meal with impeccable, friendly service, and with the restaurant's Italian flare, I figured they would be offering up a cozy Christmas atmosphere. I was all dressed up and ready to go and decided to check my email while I waited for Thomas to arrive. As I scrolled down the list in my inbox, I blinked in disbelief when I discovered I had received an email from The Dungeon! I quickly opened it and read an invitation for an in-person interview on the upcoming Tuesday evening after 6:30 p.m. Damn! What could be more of a Divine intervention than getting an offer for a job interview on Christmas Eve?

After two glasses of wine at dinner, I decided to tell Thomas about the interview. Frankly, I was feeling excited, grateful, and scared at the same time. He listened as I told him the whole story, but as soon as I finished, still full of excited energy, he started to express his concern. "Sandra, I was hoping you and I could have more of a personal dating relationship, and I'm not sure if this is a good idea." I assured him that my working at The Dungeon was not going to change me—that I was still Sandra and I would be okay. We argued. He was clearly not comfortable with the idea and, by the time we left the restaurant that evening, our potential relationship was no more. He was still supportive of me, in spite of it all, and we both agreed that our friendship was more important to us than possibly messing things up between us by dating.

Once we got back to my apartment, I was feeling more curious than ever about all things BDSM, so we opened up The Dungeon's website to do a little investigating. I had no clue about what all these beautiful Mistresses had to offer their submissive clients.

The first thing we did was open up the Mistresses' bios to read about their different specialties. I understood the easy stuff like "spanking," "corporate punishment," "bondage," and "humiliation," but, what the hell were "smothering," "CBT," "bastinado," "electro play," and "water sports"? As it turned out, Thomas knew what "smothering" was and tried to explain it to me: "Sandra, smothering is when you sit on someone with your ass to keep them from breathing." I was like, "Get the fuck out of here...it can't mean that. Surely, the women smother them with a pillow or something." But Thomas proved me wrong with a quick internet search. "Whatever," I shot back as he smiled triumphantly. "Now let's Google CBT!"

CBT, I learned, stands for Cock and Ball Torture!

I must confess that most of the images looked severe, but I was interested and curious at the same time. I looked over at the birthday boy. "Is it really possible for a woman to insert her pinky finger inside a man's penis?" I asked. Thomas never answered; he was in the fetal position on my sofa, cringing and whimpering. Funny, it didn't bother me in the least.

I suppose working in the fitness, spa, and health industry had desensitized me to matters of human anatomy. If I've seen one naked butt over my 20-year career, I've seen a million. My reaction to this sort of thing is comparable to that of a medical nurse, but our research was making Thomas a little queasy. After the online CBT education, he decided he'd had enough and said goodnight.

I'm sure that was one Christmas and birthday celebration he will never forget. I went to bed looking forward to my job interview for the following Tuesday with visions of bondage dancing in my head.

INTERVIEW DAY

I live just outside the city so the drive is usually a short one. On this night, however, I spent two solid hours in heavy traffic due to a torrential rainstorm. I can't help but appreciate how fitting it was that I drove to the infamous BDSM Dungeon for the first time on a dark and stormy night.

When I got there, I climbed the steps to find a broken-looking buzzer next to two doors. All three buttons were unmarked and there was no sign to let me know that I was even at the right place. So, with my heart pounding, I pushed all three buttons and waited. I had no idea what I was supposed to do, and the uncertainty was making me even more nervous. Then, after about a minute standing there getting soaked in the rain, one of doors buzzed and I was allowed inside.

I walked through the door and found myself at the top of a battered, paint-chipped, dimly lit staircase that appeared to lead down into the basement. Nervous and suddenly unsure, I forced myself to walk down into the gloom. After all this cloak-and-dagger stuff, I expected to hear screaming and chain rattling at the bottom—I was in a Dungeon, after all. Instead, I was surprised to be greeted by an attractive middle-aged woman.

She smiled, "Who are you?"

"Sandra LaMorgese. I'm here for a job interview."

The woman remembered my emails, and welcomed me into the parlor. The first thing I did was to ask to use the bathroom. Still insecure about my chances of being hired at my age, I had wanted to look as healthy as possible, so I drank a ton of water that afternoon to make sure that my skin would be nicely hydrated for my interview. The woman guided me through a door leading into a lounge area where the bathroom was located.

The bathroom was decent, but as I looked around in the dark lighting, I could see where the dust and dirt were building up on the plastic floor molding and tile. All I could think of while I peed was first, "Man, they love it dark around here," and second, how nice and clean I used to keep the bathroom in my wellness studio.

Whatever, I told myself, *that's the past, and I am not a snob. What do I care if The Dungeon's ladies' room has grime in the tile?* It actually seemed rather fitting.

After I checked my hair and makeup the best I could in the dim light, I made my way back to the reception area to find the woman who greeted me sitting behind a desk with a work application for me to fill out. As I sat down across from her at the desk, I reminded myself that I was determined to leave The Dungeon with a job. I had to press down firmly with the pen to help keep my hand from shaking as I filled in my name. I was actually trembling with anxiety. I kept writing, praying that the woman sitting across from me wouldn't notice how fucking scared I was.

The application was pretty basic, but when I got to the section for my birth date, I hesitated. Was it wise to reveal my true date of birth? I worried that if I answered honestly, I might get the boot for being considered too "mature." Still, I decided the truth was the best policy and jotted down my real age in the boxes with confidence. In the section asking about my special interests and abilities, I wrote yoga, outgoing personality, and excellent communication skills. I may as well have written "Virgin." They were looking for "I can use an eight-foot bullwhip, administer body piercing, and I'm a black belt in martial arts!"

I handed the woman behind the desk my completed application. She leaned back into her very high chair, lit up a cigarette, and began to read over my application. I was proud of myself for not flinching as the smoke filled the air, but I was taken aback. Smoking in the workplace (or in any public place) was something I thought we'd left far in the past—and having spent most of my professional career in the health, beauty, and wellness field made this action all the more bewildering to me. Seriously, if I lit up, I would have at least asked if the other person minded. But, as it turns out, smoking would only be the first of many things I would need to accept if I wanted to work at the BDSM Dungeon.

"Do you have any experience at all?" she asked.

I decided I'd play up the "lifestyle" Mistress persona, even though I'd only had one experience with my cub Mitchell when he pretended to be my slave. "Sure," I said with assurance. "I've been a lifestyle Mistress and Tantra practitioner for two years."

The woman flicked the ash off her cigarette. "This is not as glamorous as it might seem, you know. You'll have to work very hard. You can't get by with a pretty face."

I smiled, trying to imagine anyone describing this dark and dirty basement as glamorous, but I could talk about hard work all day. "I was a single mother. I am not afraid of hard work, and I'm willing to learn."

I could see she understood where I was coming from at this stage of the interview and I began to relax, thinking she might be considering giving me a shot at proving myself. I saw a nod, and then she started giving me the lowdown on the working conditions.

"There is absolutely no sex in any form here. No blowjobs, handjobs or footjobs. If we get busted because you had sex with a client, you get charged with a misdemeanor, and I get charged with a felony for making the appointment for you. That makes me your pimp and I go to jail. Never ever show your ass or tits to a client. You are superior to the submissive clients and slaves. If they are lucky, you may allow them to lick the bottom of your shoes."

I nodded, unsure of how to reply. Abruptly, I blurted out, "I don't hate men."

As she got up from her desk to answer a call from another room, she said, "You might after this job."

Alone in the waiting room I got the chance to look around. To my left was a wall covered with long coils of rope hanging from hooks, black leather hoods and masks, corporate beating canes, shackles, and other tools whose function I couldn't even begin to contemplate. I found it all fascinating, though, and not the least bit scary.

On the other side of the room was a huge, heavy, dark armoire and a dresser—typical dungeon furniture that you'd see in the movies. However, as creepy and dungeon-esque as it all was, on top of the dresser there was a beautifully decorated Christmas tree whose soft glow made everything in the room—yes, everything—seem warm and human. I relaxed even more.

The woman returned and told me the job was mine, with no further explanation. I wasn't about to question her decision. I was overwhelmed with gratitude for this chance to prove myself, but out loud, I just said "Thank you." She motioned for me to follow her down a dark hallway for a tour of The Dungeon's elaborate fetish rooms and torture chambers. "Come with me Sandra, I'll show you around."

THE GRAND TOUR

⬱

The first room we entered had a Zen theme. All the high walls were painted red, and mirrored. The room itself was decorated ornately in a distinctive Chinese style, including an elaborate throne, a samurai sword, beautiful etchings throughout the room—and also, adorning the grand pillars, hooks and a human suspension bar.

Moving down the hallway, she opened a second heavy wooden door, and we stepped into a torture chamber. Inside was a huge wooden rack (the kind you would shackle a slave to, circa the Middle Ages, with a wooden wheel to stretch the body out painfully and leather ties to hold the person down while the torturer used a cat o' nine tails across his back), a wooden throne, and a dark, black jail cell.

The third room was similar to the torture chamber, expect that it also had a yoke and a wheel of torture. It was much scarier. It felt like a solitary confinement cell, with stone walls and a small barred window. Even after I began working in The Dungeon full time, I refused to go into that particular room alone. After I would finish a bullwhipping or cock and ball torture session with a slave, I'd ask another Mistress to hang out with me while I straightened up the space. Rumor has it, a former slave haunts that room, and I believe it. I could sometimes feel the negative energy five feet down the hall before entering, and I wasn't the only one. We could all feel it. Sometimes the fucking music would go on by itself, or a door would slowly close. It was the creepiest part of the whole building.

The strict disciplinarian room was next. This was where the webcam is set up and the teacher holds class. The décor was sparse: a desk, a bare chalkboard, and a dunce cap on a stool in the corner. I could only imagine what kind of lessons I would be teaching.

Then, back in the hallway, the woman guided me down into a secluded area where the last two rooms were located.

One room was clearly for dress up. On one table there were a handful of mannequin heads with long blond, brunette, and auburn wigs and a 50's style make-up dresser. A tall plastic set of drawers, filled with ladies' panties, bras, and stockings stood next to a black leather sofa. A nearby closet overflowed with women's clothes, shoes, and boots in all shapes, colors, and sizes. It was everything you could ever need to make fantasies come to life.

As I entered the last room, I felt like I had walked into Dr. Frankenstein's laboratory. It was awesome! It had it all: two examining tables, suspension bars, steel intravenous poles, glass physician's cabinets filled with scary-looking medical implements, an electric chair, and a full restroom. I knew from the start I was going to enjoy working in this particular room. Thanks to my background in health and wellness, I knew I would be at ease with role play in a clinical setting.

After my tour of The Dungeon rooms, I was completely blown away...and so eager to get started.

We then worked out the details of my hours and agreed I'd start that

Friday. I needed to have chosen my "Mistress" name by then and was told to wear a short black dress that covered my tits and ass and a pair of classic six-inch pointed-toe high heels. I had two days to shop for my new fetish work clothes and decide on my new Mistress name. This was going to be fun!

I arrived for my first day of work in Midtown Manhattan and rang the bell. The door buzzed, and once again I made my way down the seedy staircase—only this time, I was carrying an overnight bag full of red lipstick, false eyelashes, a little black dress, six-inch heels, and thigh-high stockings.

When I reached the reception area, I was greeted by a different woman who yelled in a heavy German accent, "Who the fuck are you?!"

"I'm Mistress Vivian," I said, as I closed the door.

Chapter Eight

CREATING MISTRESS VIVIAN

———⊶⊷———

*"Creativity is inventing, experimenting, growing, taking risks,
breaking rules, making mistakes, and having fun."*

~MARY LOU COOK

On my first day as a dominatrix, "Who the fuck are you?"
was not the greeting I had expected, but as the front
door closed behind me, I introduced myself politely to the Head
Mistress behind the desk. She barked, "Who hired you, and do you
have any experience?"

I was speechless, and managed to shake my head no. I could sense that
this woman was not to be messed with. I couldn't tell from her accent
where she was from, maybe Germany, or Poland. It didn't matter. All
I knew was that she was terrifying, and she was angry at me.

"I have no time to train you and I would never have hired you
without any experience!" she shouted at me. Then she sighed loudly.
"Now, go into the Mistress lounge and see what you can learn from
the other experienced Dommes!"

I quickly thanked her, picked up my overnight bag and fled toward the lounge. I was relieved that she hadn't thrown me out on my ass. I tried not to let this frightening woman deter me, though. Aren't all jobs overwhelming on the first day? With this in mind, I decided to trust that after a month or so I'd be cracking the whip at The Dungeon with the best of them.

I entered the lounge, took a seat on a folding chair, and placed my bag on the floor beside me. My plan had been to observe the other women and take my cues from them, but the room was empty except for one, and she was sound asleep on a black leather sofa. I sat in silence for a few minutes, not knowing quite what to do. Then the woman woke up. "Who are you?" she asked.

I couldn't answer her right away. I was so nervous I'd forgotten my Mistress name. Finally I managed to squeak out, "I'm Sandy, but my Mistress name is Vivian." I could tell by the look she gave me that I had committed another faux pas. I later learned that the women never reveal their "other names" to each other unless they become friends outside of work.

A woman's Mistress name is a very personal thing, often imbued with meaning and private significance. It's not a choice to be taken lightly. And, like the more seasoned women, I had picked out a name that meant something to me.

I tried on Amber, Heather, and Amy, but those names felt completely wrong. I wanted an empowering name: something like Catherine,

Alexandria, or Liz. Or Scarlet. I thought of Vivien Leigh, who starred as Scarlet O'Hara in *Gone with the Wind*. I always admired her beauty, confidence, strength, weakness, and childlike vulnerability. "Vivian" felt one hundred percent right, so I made it mine.

"Alright, Vivian," said the sleepy lady on the sofa. She didn't care about why I chose the name. She was more interested in my BDSM experience.

"I've been a lifestyle Mistress for a couple years but have no professional experience," I admitted to her, adding in my little white lie. "So, I'm going to need help learning how things work around here. The woman out in the reception area just yelled at me to come in here and find someone who could help me. ...Will you help me?"

The woman, who was modestly dressed in black leggings and a tee shirt, told me she was too tired from staying up all night to be much help, and then proceeded to tell me details of her night. I was polite and listened, but only in the hope that when she finally finished her stories, she would help me get my act together. Finally, she asked, "So what are you wearing?"

It took me two solid days of shopping to find something decent. Lord and Taylor didn't carry the style I was looking for, after all. I finally found a pair of black Calvin Klein six-inch heels with open toes but, for my dress, I was going to have to think outside the box...and my age group. I found exactly what I needed—a black asymmetrical mini-dress—at Forever 21. Ironic, I thought as I stood in the checkout line.

As I showed the Mistress my new duds, she reached for my new heels. "What size shoes do you wear?"

"Ten. Why? Do you like those shoes?"

Before I knew it she had my shoes on her feet and declared, "I really like these shoes. I think I'll keep them."

Oh, really? I hadn't been in the lounge for 15 minutes and I was already being challenged! I looked at this woman straight in the eye. "I don't think so," I said. "I just spent two days looking for those shoes, and I want to keep them. Now, hand them over."

The woman smiled at me and handed them back. When she offered to show me around, I knew I had passed my first test at the Dungeon— a test from a woman who, as I soon found out, is an extremely talented and experienced Mistress in all forms of BDSM and fetish.

As we made our way around the Dungeon, we stopped in the "implement" room to take a look at all the available toys to help create a "scene." I recognized things like bullwhips, floggers, spanking paddles, collars, and leashes, but I had no idea what the other *hundreds* of items were for. Almost everything was made of either leather or steel (or both). The Mistress kept picking things up and asking me if I know how to use it. It was very clear to me that she was still busting my balls, and eventually I'd had enough. "Listen, I don't know how to use any of these things. I'm here to learn." She smiled mischievously and we moved on.

After the implement room, we headed over to where the webcam procedures take place. I had some experience with webcams from chatting with my cubs, but I had only ever watched. I'd never filmed myself. The technical procedure was a little confusing but as I watched the other Mistress do her thing I started to get the hang of it. After about an hour of training we closed the cam down, and went our separate ways.

I spent the rest of the day sitting quietly in the lounge, working on my computer and introducing myself to the other Mistresses as they came and went. All the women were pleasant and offered helpful to advice about my wardrobe, future sessions, and especially about building my portfolio. As I thought about how I wanted clients to perceive me on The Dungeon's website, I suddenly had an epiphany about creating my Mistress Vivian persona: I was a blank canvas. All I needed to do was take the dominant components of my natural personality and create my image. I could do anything I wanted.

I decided that Mistress Vivian would be an embodiment of elegant wickedness; a dark Bond girl. Mistress Vivian will charm a man with her refined beauty and style, then stick an ice pick through his heart even as he professes his loyalty to her.

Every actor wants to play the bad guy once in a while because it gives us a chance to go into the dark side of ourselves and expand our range. I remember musing with my friend John after I had become settled in my role as a Mistress: "Is there really much of a difference between what I do at the Dungeon and what Angelina Jolie does in her action movies? We're both playing strong, sexy, powerful, dominant, kickass woman." John agreed, laughing and nodding somewhat incredulously.

When I finally finished my online portfolio for Mistress Vivian, it read:

> *Mistress Vivian is a ProDomme and Fetishist. She is an intelligent, educated, tall, elegant beauty. She is exactly what you want in a woman: blonde hair, green eyes, an hourglass figure, and beautiful polished feet that are perfect for trampling and smothering all over you if you misbehave.*

> *She has beautiful, agile hands that will not hesitate to whip you into shape, and her flawless skin is unmarred by tattoos or piercings.*

> *Her extensive background in the sensual and erotic arts (Tantric) provides Mistress Vivian with that extra edge. Her formal training in acting and modeling makes her the perfect Mistress for extreme self-expression and role play.*

Voilà

Once I figured out the dominant, dark, and dangerously alluring attitude, it was time to work on my outside image. However, this step proved to be much more difficult than I thought it would be. At first I had resisted making myself up. I'm not used to fussing with my hair and makeup, and honestly I feel attractive in my natural state. *But I'm not working in my natural state,* I reminded myself. *I'm working in a fantasy world.* So, I changed my way of thinking and started watching the other women do their makeovers—and I asked for lots of help.

DAILY TRANSFORMATION

꙳

G rowing up, I was a tomboy. I preferred climbing trees, swinging from a Tarzan rope, skipping rocks in the creek, skateboarding, or kickball to any of the typical girly activities. Not much has changed since then. I rarely wear makeup on my personal time, usually have my hair in a ponytail, and can typically be seen wearing my favorite comfy yoga pants and carrying my dusty hiking backpack. I suppose that's why my girlfriend Serena was so stunned when she accompanied me on a BDSM photo shoot at the Dungeon. She was shocked to meet my alter ego, Mistress Vivian.

Photo shoots are essential to marketing my business. They're also a lot of fun. I want to give potential clients a sense of my range, from my darker personality to my down-to-earth playfulness. I have many "newbie" clients who seek me out specifically for my "vanilla" look. It lessens the fear factor for them. I always find it humorous that most clients expect me to be on the "sweeter" side due to my warm persona. I tell them, "That's how I lure you in, with my beautiful face and sweet charm." Then I haul off and knee them straight in the balls, or (if I *am* actually feeling sweet) I might pull their head back by their hair and spit in their face. They love it.

We arrived for the shoot around 2 p.m. on a Sunday afternoon. Before Serena walked down the staircase, I advised her to wait while I asked the other Mistresses for their approval. I didn't see Serena's visit as an issue, but I learned quickly all the Mistresses have respect for each other's privacy, and I would never bring an outsider into the environment without clearing it first with everyone. Once I had the okay, I brought Serena down into our subculture of bondage, discipline, sadism, and masochism.

First, I introduced her to the Head Mistress and the other women, and then we took a tour of the fetish rooms and torture chambers. Serena seemed intrigued and titillated by the entire experience. I mean, really, who wouldn't be? I believe we all have a bit—or a lot—of voyeurism in us, which would explain the multimillion-dollar porn industry and the countless reality shows on mainstream television. Although we may not engage in alternative lifestyles, we love to watch other people doing it. Once I dragged Serena out of the last chamber, we settled into the Mistress lounge area so that I could create Mistress Vivian for the photographer.

Although my locker is situated in a room adjacent to the lounge, Serena could clearly see me from her leather chair. I had been working at the Dungeon for a year and was very comfortable with the routine that transformed my reflection in the full-length mirror across from the locker door: hair first, then dress, boots, and finally makeup. As I went through my makeover, Serena relaxed and started to chat with the other women. Every once in a while she looked over to include me in the conversation as I curled my hair.

When I slipped on my skintight fetish dress, the dialogue between us shifted completely. "Oh my God, Sandra," Serena exclaimed. "You have breasts and an awesome, sexy body!"

I laughed and replied, "My body was always here—I just never wore tight or revealing clothes at the wellness studio or when I hang out with friends."

For the rest of time it took me to adjust my classic fetish dress on my curves, glue on false eyelashes, draw on black eye-liner tips, and apply a generous amount of red lipstick, Serena never took her eyes off me. "So, this is Mistress Vivian," she said when the finishing touches were done. "I've heard so much about you. It's my pleasure to finally meet you, Mistress."

EVERY JOB HAS ITS QUIRKS, RIGHT?

ead Mistress Barbara was a royal pain in the ass. Every time I turned around, she was on my back about something. During my first week at The Dungeon, it was my red lipstick. My lips were dry and cracked from a head cold that had come on suddenly, and I kept licking them for moisture, smearing my lipstick in the process. I tried to explain, but she didn't want to hear it. "Fix your lipstick!!" she yelled every time I walk passed the front desk.

Then she turned her attention to my wardrobe. Every day I brought something from home to wear and every day she yelled, "No! You need fetish clothes! Leather, PVC, latex, six-inch pointed-toe heels! And color your hair blonde! Clients want blondes!"

I wanted to take her advice but I only had about $200 in my checking account. Spending the last of my money on fetish clothes would be a huge leap of faith, but there's something about standing in a BDSM dungeon that really changes your perspective. After all, why pick up a bullwhip if you don't intend to use it? I wanted to be there and had already invested in my goal, so why hold back now? "Head Mistress Barbara, where can I buy fetish clothes?"

I'm not in Kansas anymore, I thought as I walked into the fetish store Head Mistress Barbara had told me about. The clothing racks had a few "costumes" of sexy nurse outfits and schoolgirl skirts, but mostly the shelves and racks were full of black leather and shiny PVC. Exactly what I needed. I thumbed through the dresses and found a classic black, below the knee, low-cut, corset dress that laced up the back. It was very sexy and fit the look I was trying to achieve. When I put it on, I felt confident and hot. It was perfect.

As I stood at the counter to pay, I remembered some very good advice Mistress Deborah had given me on my second day at The Dungeon: "You're a beautiful mature woman and you're going to be very busy because there are no other Mistresses here with your brand. Don't waste your time on trying to compete with the younger girls and what they're wearing. Wear what brings out your own uniqueness." Mistress Deborah was so right. Women are sexy and beautiful at every age and I wanted to thoroughly experience and express my sexuality at my honest age of 55. Why are we so hell bent on trying to be younger anyway?

I walked eagerly back to the Dungeon to show Head Mistress Barbara my new fetish dress. When I arrived she was already yelling at me. "Get dressed! You have a client coming in for a requested session in 30 minutes and I have to train you in how to do an over-the-knee spanking!" Damn! I couldn't believe it! Someone had actually asked for me? I was so thrilled and grateful to have my first client. I'd even make back the money I'd spent on the fetish dress!

I hurried into the Mistress lounge and grabbed my overnight bag to begin my transformation. The whole time I was getting ready Head Mistress Barbara was right behind me, frantically explaining how to properly spank someone. "How hard can it be?" I asked. "I take my hand and smack the guy's ass."

Mistress Barbara was not pleased with that response. She called another Mistress over (the ball-busting sleepy-eyed one, of course) and demanded she be my guinea pig. The whole ordeal was making me nervous and I began to sweat off the makeup I was applying. My new dress was dripping with perspiration. Finally, I told her, "Listen, you're going to have to trust me at some point. It's a spanking, not a full body suspension."

Mistress Barbara did not agree. A minute later, I was practicing on Sleepy's ass.

ALL EMPLOYEES MUST WASH THEIR HANDS BEFORE RETURNING TO WORK

I led my client into a fetish room to start the session. My nerves were steady. More than anything, I felt relieved to be away from my spanking crash-course. I spent 10 minutes with my client, listening as he described how he envisioned the play between us. I was mommy, he said, and he had been a very bad boy at school and needed to be punished.

Great! Let's do it! I was grateful that my first session was relatively relaxed and simple with an easy-going client. When we started, what surprised me most was how difficult it was to keep my own emotions out of it. I had to work hard to keep my true self out of the session. I reminded myself that I was not his mommy—I was just playing a part—and that one identity had nothing to do with the other. I shook my head vigorously in an attempt shake off thoughts about mommies smacking their sons.

The wooden chair where all this was playing out was just a few feet from sliding glass closet doors, so I couldn't help but to observe the scene as I was disciplining my *bad boy*. He was naked, lying across my knees. I was thankful for my long black dress—and also thankful for the reflective glass, which allowed me to check out how nice my legs looked in the dress.

My client spent the next 50 minutes over my knee as I spanked him with my bare hand and reprimanded him for his bad behavior in class. Though he pleaded and begged me to forgive him, I never did. When I was finished, my client's ass was cherry red and he felt wonderfully happy. My aching hands did not. *I guess it's not all glamorous*, I thought as I blew on them lightly. Since then, I've learned to protect my poor hands by using a paddle and a lot more role play. This way, the client has an enjoyable experience, and so do I.

SANDRA, MEET VIVIAN.
VIVIAN, MEET SANDRA.

Working in fantasy has uncovered new realities for me. As I've worked to develop my persona, I've realized new truths about my actual identity. I've taken my own personality traits and exaggerated them. Played with them. Aestheticized them. Sandra certainly exists within Mistress Vivian. I'm not really a woman who sits around all day petting a Persian cat as slaves fan me round the clock, of course, but my Mistress personality creates that illusion in a powerful way. And, when the illusion is complete, the confidence, strength, and sexual energy of that scene stay with me after I'm finished with it. Mistress Vivian is also a part of Sandra.

In order to create Mistress Vivian, I had to acknowledge the places where she already existed within me and be true to them. I had to honor my desire to be dominant instead of suppressing it. I had to embrace my real age and real figure—Mistress Vivian is not a 50-year-old trying to look like she's 25. I had to love myself so that Mistress Vivian could be worshipped. I had to feel good so that my clients could feel pleasure.

Time and time again clients have told me, "I love seeing you laugh. When you're laughing, I know you're having fun too." I believe this is at the core of why my clients enjoy my services and why they can't stop coming back for more. My positive feelings about myself fill the room, and they are contagious. And really, who could get tired of that?

Chapter Nine

LESSONS I LEARNED THROUGH BDSM

—⁂—

"If you judge people, you have no time to love them."

~MOTHER TERESA

I spent most of my first 55 years getting myself ready to be happy. I can remember thinking, *I'm not ready to be in a loving relationship. I'm not emotionally ready. I need to finish college first, and I need to be financially secure.* The truth is, I believed that if I did enough to improve myself or control my life, I would be more lovable and more loving—that I would finally deserve the relationship I was trying to convince myself I didn't want.

I could not have been more wrong. I *do* desire self-awareness, new experiences, and the peace of mind that comes with financial independence, I understand now that being lovable and loving has nothing to do with *being improved upon* or with *getting more things done.* We go through our entire lives developing, experiencing, and growing, but I discovered over the past four years that love, happiness, joy, and compassion do not come through doing and improving—instead, they come through being and feeling.

Tantra opened me up to learning how to love myself. It taught me to understand that my birthright, my purpose, is to be loving, passionate, happy, joyful, healthy, wealthy, compassionate, and trusting *just as I am now*. Later, BDSM opened up my awareness even more, showing me that others are worthy of the same love, passion, happiness, joy, health, wealth, compassion, and trust as well. *Just as they are now.*

The Dungeon was an extreme learning environment, to be sure, but during my time there I have learned to truly accept other people with an open mind and an open heart. By practicing BDSM, I've come to understand that people are different and have very different desires, sexualities, hopes, dreams, loves, purposes, ambitions, and styles. And all of it is good. In the very beginning, I had to ask myself: If something or someone brings us genuine joy, happiness, pleasure, and love, how can that be wrong?

We tend to judge people who are *different* from ourselves. We say things like,

> *"Look at the way he wears his hair."*

> *"She's such a slut; just look at the way she dresses."*

> *"Carnivores are such savages."*

> *"Republicans are idiots."*

> *"Democrats are ruining this country."*

Every one of these judgments is just another way of saying: *If you're not like ME, then you're wrong.*

I could not have chosen a better occupation to teach me to become less judgmental and to embrace natural human curiosity—to simply *have* experiences, and not judge them. I never would have expected it, but my job as a Domme taught me, above all else, how to have compassion for myself and for others.

CRANKING UP THE HEAT

A s I continued training with the more experienced Mistresses, the sessions became significantly more intense. At The Dungeon, the final say about any session always belongs to the Mistress. If I go into a consultation with a client and decide I'm not interested in working with them, I simply say, "No." The management stands by us and honors a Mistress's wishes over any client's request. Even so, during my training, it seemed like the other women were trying to find out exactly what I was made of— trying to push me to the farthest limits of my comfort zone, and then just a little bit further.

One day, I heard the Head Mistress screaming my name down the hall in her usual screechy voice, "Viv!" I ran into the parlor, assuming from her urgency that the building was on fire. "What is it?" I asked. The Head Mistress abruptly stopped her yelling and whispered in my ear, "Start drinking water, you're going to need to 'potty' in thirty minutes."

What?

I'd never peed on anyone before. I couldn't even imagine how to go about doing such a thing. Frankly, I couldn't even imagine the type of person who wants to be peed on by a complete stranger. I paused for a moment, working hard to set aside the judgments that were already popping up in my head. Then, after about 10 minutes of downing as much water as I could, I asked the Head Mistress for instructions.

"Hey, Barb. My bladder is as full as a water balloon. But, exactly how do I—I mean, how would you like me to, uh... well, you know!"

Mistress Barb laughed as if this is the funniest thing she'd ever heard. "You've never peed on anyone before?"

I wasn't amused. I stood up straight as though I were world-class at this sort of thing. "Sure, I mean, of course I have…. I was just wondering about the procedure here at The Dungeon. Naturally, I want to follow protocol."

Barb appeared to buy my lame cover-up and ran through it with me.

"The session Mistress will call you in about 15 minutes before the session is over. The client will be lying on the floor on top of puppy training pads. The session Mistress will let you know if you should have him drink it or if you should just pee on his cock and ball. After the client leaves, it would nice if you could go in and ask her if she needs any help cleaning up. However, the cleanup is unusually done by the client. After all, he is the slave."

Once she gave me the drip-by-drip details, she added, "Don't worry about it too much. 99% percent of the time the guys just want to try to get a look at your pussy."

Oh. My. *God.*

The 30 minutes I had to wait before entering the session room were the longest I had ever experienced. I sat in the lounge drinking from a liter bottle of water, squirming from the discomfort of a full bladder and trying to get my head around what I was about to do. Outside of work, I am a woman who always pees with the door shut. Hell, the idea of peeing in public bathrooms with multiple stalls made me uncomfortable, let alone peeing on another human being! I believe some things should just remain private, and moving one's bowels and urinating *in front of a stranger* are at the top of the list. I wasn't even sure if I could mentally relax enough to do it. There was a larger issue too: I'd be exposing my private parts. Exposing myself!

I nearly backed out. I was thinking, *This is crazy—there's no way I can do this.* I was ready to tell the Head Mistress that urinating for money was against my belief system just to get out of it.

Then it came to me: I would wear my long fetish dress. With the dark lighting in the chamber room and me in a below-the-knee dress, he wouldn't see a thing. It was the perfect solution to keep him from having a clear view. With that resolved, I felt a little better. Then I heard my name being called from down the hall.

Showtime.

As I entered the chamber, I felt my attitude had suddenly switched from fear to acceptance. The client was in position on the hard cement floor, which was layered with puppy pads. I was grateful that the other Mistress was in the chamber with me, and I relaxed enough to squeeze out a few drops. There were no feelings of negative judgment in the air. The only feelings that surrounded me were from power exchange and sexual energy. I closed my eyes, wrapped the atmosphere of intense trust in the room around me like a blanket, and let go.

FEELING "IN THE FLOAT"

That feeling of focus, acceptance, and emotional release is what we Mistresses referred to as being "in the float." The first time I ever heard the phrase used was during one of my bull-whipping and flogging training sessions with another beautiful, confident, and extremely talented Mistress whose client was very submissive to her, and therefore agreeable to being part of my training.

Mistress Alex beat her slave's back and ass with various whips and floggers to demonstrate the safest areas on the body to be beaten. Precision is necessary to avoid striking or wrapping the leather around certain parts of the body that could potentially damage a vital organ. After about 20 minutes of demonstration, Mistress Alex handed me the flogger and advised, "Stand up straight, be confident. You're the one who is in control."

The slave, who was tied up between two pillars with his legs and arms spread out in an X, continued to thank his Mistress for allowing him to help with my training, and to praise her and her extraordinary beauty.

I took the flogger in my hand. I whirled it once or twice to get a feel for the weight of the leather tassels. I adjusted my distance as if I were about to hit a tennis ball, getting into a safe and comfortable position while also intimidating the slave with the sound of the swirling leather. Typically, I give a few "warm-up" lashes before using all my power and force to strike the slave's body, but since the other Mistress had been whipping him already in her demonstration, I felt confident that he was already warmed up, anticipating and desiring a powerful stroke. I stepped in and fired the first blow on his back. Mistress Alex was impressed with my natural athletic abilities and encouraged me to continue.

After 10 minutes of the beating, Mistress Alex circled the room. "Do you have time to stay for another hour?" she asked me. There are a few more things I want to show you." She stepped in closer and whispered in my ear, "We're now in the float. Can you feel the energy?"

I'd never heard the term, but I did feel the energy. It felt good, like a natural high. "I'd love to stay!" I told her.

DON'T THINK I'VE FORGOTTEN ABOUT YOGA...

My time at The Dungeon also gave me new insights into energy, which had been one of my strongest interests ever since I began studying yoga and, more specifically, Tantra. Since many people have not studied these topics extensively, I will offer a brief overview here.

In eastern Indian *ayurvedic* literature, the silence that comes through meditation is known as *Shakti* (the feminine) and the energy current is *Shiva* (the masculine). When we marry the masculine and feminine together during meditation—or BDSM—in order to quiet the mind, we create internalized energy and emotion, opening ourselves up to a higher awareness and direct communion with the Divine.

The *Kundalini Shakti* is the coiled, dormant potential life force energy in every human, and it has seven energy portals. These portals, known as *chakras,* run from the base of the spine to the crown of the head. According to Eastern philosophy, each of the seven chakras must be open and balanced for enlightenment and full self-expression, including expression of our sexuality.

THE FIRST CHAKRA: A four-petal red lotus located at the base of the spine by the perineum. It represents earth, peace, and serenity, the solidity that we call the "physical world" along with our survival instincts for safety and security. In order for us to awaken and explore other areas of our expression and wholeness, we must first be rooted, grounded, and feel safe and secure.

It may sound silly to think of The Dungeon as a safe place, but that's exactly what it was for me. The financial income I generated by being a professional dominatrix allowed me to relax and live in peace, knowing I could pay my bills and sleep in a safe, warm bed every night. Until we feel grounded and secure, it is nearly impossible to explore our creativity or to truly enjoy life.

THE SECOND CHAKRA: Traveling up the spine, we find the six-petal chakra lotus located in the pelvis, sacrum, and hips. This chakra represents water, as well as bliss, longing, passion, pleasure, sensation, and desire. It governs all the sensual aspects of our lives, including sex.

The dual nature of sex is freely explored in BDSM. Most people who are looking for a dominant partner (professional or personal) are naturally dominant people themselves and want to have the submissive experience. Similarly, a naturally submissive person usually seeks a submissive partner (professional or personal) for the experience of being dominant. A CEO who spends her days making important decisions and running the world may desire her partner to take control in her personal life. A man who has to follow strict rules at work without offering input may want to experience expression through dominating his partner. The forces are complimentary, a dynamic system of yin and yang between partners.

THE THIRD CHAKRA: Moving upward into the solar plexus is the yellow, ten-petal lotus that signifies our burning purpose and awakens our self-empowerment and will.

I am a Type A personality, which could mean that I have an overactive third chakra—a perfect arrangement for a Dominatrix. Telling my clients what to do, when to do it, and how I want it done feels very natural to me. In these consensual power exchange sessions, I have the opportunity to express this energy in a healthy manner.

THE FOURTH CHAKRA: We find the green twelve-petal lotus chakra at the heart center, symbolizing freedom, lightness, and love. The heart chakra embraces the awakening of the Divine spirit, which helps the heart to unlock and be free from pride and ego. Once we experience the lightheartedness of self-love we can delve into the mystery of loving relationships with others. The heart is a soft, compassionate place of connection; opening up the heart to love enables us not only to balance the mind, body, and spirit, but also to embrace an attitude of service toward others.

The most important keys to my personal development have been self-love, self-worth, free will, and understanding who I really am. My clients are able to grow in these areas as well, by acting on their true desires and playfully engaging with their sexual selves. We are open to one another at all times, and we exchange positive energy that benefits both of us in the end. Once I realized this truth, I became free of my internal and external judgments, and this freedom opened my heart to loving myself and others.

THE FIFTH CHAKRA: This chakra is a blue lotus with sixteen petals of "understanding." Because the fifth chakra is located in the throat, it is the chakra that governs all communication, speaking, hearing, listening, and creative expression. It helps us to understand our inner truth and to use our voice to convey that truth to the outside world. Communication before, during, and after a BDSM or Fetish session is crucial to the success or failure of the experience. The first thing I say to a potential client during a phone consultation is, "Don't be shy. I am the person you can be completely honest with in regards to your fantasy or fetish. I am not judgmental, and when you explain to me who you are and what you desire, I can determine if we are a match in 'edge pushing' and 'hard limits' in session play."

Many times, I will be contacted by men who, for the first time in their entire lives, are expressing their desires and feelings out loud to another person. This is where empathic communication on my part comes into play. Even if the desires and fantasies cross one of my boundaries, I still show respect by saying, "Although you seem sincere, this would not be a session I'd be interested in." However, if everything is agreeable to both me and the potential client, we move on to the scheduling phase.

Before I begin with the bondage, head hoods, and duct tape, I need to know if my client has any physical limitations or phobias, such as claustrophobia. The last thing I want to do is clause any suffering that wasn't planned or, worse, permanent damage. If a client has had shoulder surgery in the past, I'm not going to hogtie him; if he gets manic while holding his breath, I'm not going to hold his head under water.

During the session with a client, I rely mostly on body language and non-verbal communication. Did you know that over 90% of the messages we receive from other people are through non-verbal communication? If my client so much as moves his fingers, I start to wonder if the ropes or shackles are too tight, and I immediately ask about his comfort level. Of course, the one sure-fire sign that a client is having a good time is an erection. A hard cock never lies.

Afterwards, communication is key to bringing the client physically and emotionally out of his emotional state of submission, or "sub space." This transition can be very intense for some clients who still struggle with shame and guilt about their sexuality. At the end of the session, I usually ask the client, "How are you feeling?" as I am untying him, and then we discuss the session's pros and cons in a relaxed conversational tone.

Freedom of self-expression and the freedom to trust are the foundations of authentic and healthy communication.

THE SIXTH CHAKRA: An indigo two-petal lotus located in the brow, called the "Third Eye." The Third Eye represents the core of vision, insight, visualization, intuition, imagination, and telepathy.

One of the first questions I'm asked when I tell someone about my career choice is, "Aren't you afraid of what could happen to you?" I understand how someone may worry about the safety of working so intimately with another person, but I assure them, "I follow my instincts 100%." I never ignore red flags, and when something doesn't feel right, I stop. My clients also understand that if our session moves beyond either of our personal boundaries, it needs to stop immediately. All animals instinctively know whether they are safe or in danger, and human beings are no exception.

The Seventh Chakra: Finally, we travel up to the crown of the head where the white or violet lotus of a thousand petals resides. This chakra connects us to the "Divine." Those with a healthy, balanced crown chakra have attained serenity, trust in God, the self, and the Universe, and they are free from ego-driven desires. They strive for perceptivity, wisdom, trust, selflessness, and purposeful lives.

Dealing with Stigma

I was raised a Baptist—saved and baptized, the whole nine yards. I actually loved attending the tent revivals and listening to gospel music, and I still do. I remember when I was a young girl I used to sneak off with a girlfriend to an all-black church in the small town where I lived, and we'd sit up in the balcony for hours listening to the preacher and the testimonial gospel choir. It was awesome! Growing up, we attended church every Sunday, said grace before meals, and prayed before bedtime. Always wary of sudden overnight death and the fate of our eternal souls, we prayed the classic prayer each night:

Now I lay me down to sleep,

I pray the Lord my soul to keep.

If I should die before I wake,

I pray the Lord my soul to take.

As a little girl, I was happy to comply in order to wash all my sins away so that God would be sure to have me.

It was only when I began seeing the world differently that I could reflect on how my entire life had been spent living with the fear that God judged me as a sinner. This is not unusual. Many of us receive the "sinner stigma" before we even speak our first words. That's what infant christening is for: to cleanse us of our sins and wash them away.

What I've discovered, though, is that God is not some old, white-bearded man sitting on a throne and looking down on me, constantly determining if I'm worthy or not. I now believe God created me in His/Her/Its image and pure essence, not the other way around. That, as a pure source, God is *unconditional love, supreme intelligence, and unbreakable connection*, and is therefore incapable of judgment against me.

I also believe God intends my free will to be spontaneous with my individual choices, so I'm not subjected to any enforced regulations. Really, aren't our triumphs and failures how we learn and transcend? Therefore, if this is the Truth of who I am—a "part" of God—then, as individual as I am, I remain a part of the Whole.

Or, to put it very simply, I am at peace with myself spiritually, emotionally, mentally, and physically—obtaining true optimal health. I can never hope to achieve this state while denying myself something as fundamental as self-expression, intimacy, and self-love.

FINDING BALANCE AND OWNING MY PERSONAL PREFERENCES

A nother important realization (which I reached early on, but have continued to grow in my understanding of for years now) is that BDSM isn't a practice of rejection, anger, hate, or punishment. It's a giving practice of love, compassion, and acceptance. I always tell my clients, "I'm not in the pain business; I'm in the pleasure business." BDSM is an expression of the totality of both the dominance and submission. Furthermore, the only way such acts can be expressed is through trust, communication, and respect, and by honoring ourselves and our partners in the present moment. This is exactly what Tantra teaches.

Along with my training in the Dungeon, I also attended various BDSM workshops (Fire Play, Communication/Interrogation, Hypnotizing, Hot Wax, Bullwhipping, Rope Suspension, Bondage) throughout the city. Although there are numerous workshops and trainings in the BDSM community, the more experienced Dommes recommended that I specialize rather than try to be a jack-of-all-trades. My specialty turned out—somewhat unsurprisingly, considering my acting background—to be "role playing" with incorporation of other modalities. I was the "twisted" cougar, teacher, doctor, boss, secret agent, aunt, mommy, step-mother, and through it all, a dominatrix.

The first workshop I attended was on "Sensual Knife Play." The couple demonstrating the knife play had clearly been doing this together for a while. The male "top" (dominant) laid the nude female "bottom" (submissive) on a massage table in front of the class and one by one he ran various knives up and down her body, focusing on her nipples, pussy, and throat. During the demonstration, he taught us how to "safely" play with knives for excitement and a few scratches, but without permanent injury. As I watched the couple, noting their unique style and techniques, I realized that I didn't have to do *everything* I learned in class to have fun and incorporate different physical components to my scenes—I could make my job, and all the play I incorporated in my sessions—entirely my own.

I love bringing the power and energy play to life in my sessions, and I typically incorporate knife play (if applicable) during the first session with a client. Once I have him in a good position, I hold a knife up against his balls, or maybe his throat. (Keep in mind that, in our first session together, the man won't know me well, so when he hears the knife open, he won't be sure if I'm crazy enough to really hurt him.) That's exactly where I want him—in the float of uncertainty—and, every time, that's exactly where the client loves to be as well.

One of my favorite knife play scenes is to bind the slave into an old fashioned "yoke." It's the same sort of apparatus used in the Salem Witch Trials. My client bends over and places his head and hands in the three holes in the wood and then I clamp it shut. Once my slave is immobilized in the yoke, I pull back his cock and balls around his ass with rope for full exposure, and then fasten up my strap-on (which the slave can't see, because I stand behind him). I click the blade open and slowly run the knife down the slave's spine, ass, the shaft of his cock and across both balls. The whole time, I half-whisper to him, "Don't move, and don't even breathe. Accidents do happen and I'm sure you don't want your next move to be in the hospital." It's amazing how still someone can be.

After I've made my point to the slave, I slowly walk around to the front of the yoke so that he can be surprised by the sight of me wearing the strap-on and holding the knife.

"Well, well. You sure have gotten yourself into quite a predicament, haven't you?" I say.

"Yes, Mistress."

"Hmmmm, what to do with you? I'll tell you what. You can decide your own fate."

"Yes, Mistress."

"Here are your choices: You can either have both of your balls cut off, OR you can suck my cock. What's it going to be?"

"I guess I'll suck your cock, Mistress."

And he does.

As wild as such a scene may seem, remember that in all types of play, there MUST be a preexisting foundation of trust, communication, and respect—the kind that I establish individually with each of my clients. When we first meet, they tell me what they want and what their hard limits are, and I communicate my own. Then, and only then, can we both enjoy ourselves and the experience. The BDSM code is "Safe, Sane, and Consensual," and everyone in the room respects this agreement before, during, and after the play.

SPEAKING MY MIND

One of the hardest parts of learning to be a dungeon Mistress was mastering verbal humiliation towards slaves. The physical torture was easy in comparison, and I had a hard time calling a slave "a worthless piece of shit" or telling a slave "you're not worth the scum off the bottom of my shoes." In the beginning, I felt bad for speaking to people like that, but this sort of verbal domination is often just as important as the physical play for creating the right atmosphere, and eventually, I got the hang of it.

Once, I locked a slave in the jail cell and told him that I had been walking in slave sweat and cum all day and needed the soles of my shoes licked clean. "If you ever intend to be released from that cell, you had better clean the slave sweat and cum off my shoes, you pathetic fucking loser!" I sneered.

He heisted for a second, as if to wonder whether I'd really been walking through such things all day, but then proceeded to lick the soles of my shoes clean anyway. It was part of what he wanted from our exchange.

On another occasion, a slave said to me "Can I speak, Mistress?"

"Yes, what is it?" I asked with eyes rolling.

"If it will amuse you, you can be meaner to me," he said.

The Dungeon is an "extreme atmosphere of sadomasochism in forms of physiological humiliation and physical torture" and then some, and the fantasies created there have almost nothing to do with the everyday lives that the Mistresses and clients lead. Ironically, though, this radical environment was a perfect training ground for me to learn to push my boundaries and take risks out in the real world. For instance, once I was able to confidently dress up a client in a bra and panties, thigh-high tights, and high heels and make him do cheerleading calls out in the parlor area for the Head Mistress, the thought of going to the movies alone no longer intimidated me. After learning to shout at and insult my slaves at work, I no longer feared having to turn down the cashiers at stores when they pressed me to open rewards cards. I learned confidence and assertiveness in the extreme as a dominatrix, which gave me the perspective and ability to stand up for myself and take risks in my everyday life.

HOW THE OTHER HALF LIVES

When I was hired at the Dungeon, I made it clear that I was only interested in being a Domme and not in doing professional submissive work or sweaty wrestling matches (even though they paid quite a bit more). A professional submissive, or a Mistress who switches back and forth naturally between dominant and submissive roles, offers her clients the option of being the dominant player in the scene. I have a lot of respect for "subs," as they're much more trusting and more natural receivers then dominants. Believe me when I say, these ladies can take a beating like a man!

One of the Mistresses with whom I was close at The Dungeon is a "switch"—an extremely beautiful, sexy, stylish, and smart woman who also happens to enjoy getting a good beating every so often. The first time she showed me the lash marks on her abdomen, back, ass, and legs after a personal D/s scene, I felt protective of her and questioned the seriousness of the beating. "Ally, are you sure you're okay with this?" I asked anxiously. She just looked at me and smiled. "Don't worry Vivian, this is not my first rodeo."

I could not see myself enjoying a scenario where I crawled around on the floor in girly lingerie while a client insisted that I call him "Sir" or "Master" and spanked me. I'm not judging, but it's just not me, and my friend Ally agreed. "Vivian, I've been working in this industry for 10 years and I have never seen any Mistress take to this business as fast as you have. You totally get it—but you are not submissive."

One afternoon, however, I had the opportunity to experience what I'd avoided so far. One of the younger male clients asked the Head Mistress if I'd be interested in having a submissive scene with him. She came to me with his request. "I don't know how well I'll handle it," I told her, "but I'm willing to try."

I went into the consultation room with the client who explained his fantasy. "I want you to play my older naughty secretary who has a sexual desire to be with me. And I will let you keep your job if you do as you're told."

Oh, brother, I thought. I already felt ridiculous just thinking about playing this part. On the other hand, I really wanted to see if there was any possibility that I'd come around and enjoy it. *What the hell?* I figured. It was only 60 minutes.

Within the first few minutes of the scene, I realized that my acting talents were going to make a big difference in my ability to get through the session. The client verbally humiliated me, spanked me with a leather paddle, and worked some serious power play for the entire 60 minutes. I headed for the lounge afterwards with a red, sore, bruised ass. "How was it?" Ally asked, but one look at my face told the story. "That bad, huh?"

I nodded. "I think I'm going to stick to my dominant side from now on."

For a week after the session, the Head Mistress applied some sort of ointment on my ass to relieve the redness and bruises. Slowly, they faded, and I was back to normal, except that even after the bruises were gone, I couldn't get the dynamic of dominant-and-submissive out of my head. After a while, I began to wonder if the power play between the two had something to do with why my personal relationships never lasted.

DOMINANCE AND SUBMISSION
IN REAL LIFE

~

I'm attracted to dominating men. I always have been. With my
new experiences of dominant-and-submissive power and energy
play, however, I understand how I may have been fighting Mother
Nature all along by banging heads with another dominant personality
for control.

I'm not easy for most men to handle: I'm independent, driven,
passionate, confident, and I do what I want to do—now more than
ever. In addition, any man in my life needs to accept my desire for
"wiggle room" but still believe at the end of the day that I'll eagerly
come home to him. After my brief foray into the world of "subs,"
however, I made a change in my personal relationships: I decided to
relax and go with my submission flow now and then to balance out
the power dynamics. What I discovered, to my amazement, was that
I'd been missing out on more intimate and loving relationships by
not being able to relax, enjoy, and receive.

Even though I accepted this intellectually, the thought of enacting
this kind of submission still made me bristle. I wasn't sure how I felt
about letting a man be in charge, even for a little bit. *Will it be like my
icky client experience?* I worried. With this apprehension in mind, I
decided to start exploring my submissive side slowly. The first thing
I tried was treating my male friends as special guests whenever they

came over, with a *How can I please you?* and *Is everything to your liking?* kind of attitude.

"Can I get you a drink?" I'd ask. "Are you comfortable?" Before too long, I could see how much I was enjoying the effort of pampering, serving, and pleasing him. After spending such a long time bolstering and relishing in my dominant side, I was pleasantly surprised by how much I enjoyed exploring my submissive side as well.

One afternoon, a long-time girlfriend and I went out for drinks to watch the NFL playoffs. A man I was dating met up with us halfway through the game. To me, it seemed like I was behaving like my usual self (dominant and the center of attention) around the two of them, but the next day my friend commented, "I saw a side of you last night that I never saw before. As soon as that man walked in the room, your personality changed completely. I saw a softer and more relaxed side of you"

I'm not suggesting that I've become a doormat—not by any means. I still hold my ground with men and do my own thing, and as of yet I can't be found in the kitchen slaving away or buying into domestic duties. I do, however, feel more of a balance between dominance and submission in my attitude and in my relationships, and this balance brings me happiness. I'm changing, and right now, the change works for me.

I suppose I have always understood the relationship between dominance and submission from the times in my life when I've worked with people who are experts in their fields, from personal fitness trainers to coaches, and television directors to photographers. In these situations, I relax in the trusting relationship, allowing myself to be guided or doing as I'm told. That's why I have such people in my life—so I don't have to learn and do things alone. I trust that they have my best interests at heart. If I can be submissive with strangers, then, why not submit in a loving, trusting personal relationship and explore new possibilities for becoming more intimate?

I know for a fact that there are many people with secret submissive and dominant self-expression desires, who wish their partners would be more understanding and open to a more non-conventional relationship. In fact, most of my clients are happily married men who adore their wives and children, but who have no opportunity to experiment with their sexuality. They come to me because there is no sex involved in the sessions (they don't want to sexually cheat on their partners) and because I am open and nonjudgmental about their self-expression of submission. Almost 100% of my clients in monogamous relationships have told me, "I wish my wife was open to this" or "There is no way my partner will ever understand my desires."

I am genuinely glad for these men who are honest with themselves about their deepest desires. Natural desires may be swept under the rug temporarily, but sooner or later they will surface. I say, instead of trying to suppress our desires, why not embrace them and open up to a life of freedom?

FINDING THE COURAGE TO LIVE AUTHENTICALLY

꙳

A ll of our decisions come from either fear or love. Opening up about self-expressive behaviors is always, *always* scary, and actively pursuing personal desires takes courage. Professionally, I have this self-expression thing down, but personally? Well, I am still taking baby steps when it comes to risk-taking. Not too long ago I was cuddling with a lover one morning when he asked, "What's the kinkiest thing you ever did?" I lay on the bed, thinking. *Vivian has gotten into some kinky shit, I mused, but Sandy?...She has very little experience.*

I still don't have much. More importantly, though, I have learned to be open and to communicate my feelings and desires. I have identified my hard limits. I know myself better than ever before, and, more recently, I have started to unpack some of the deep fears and desires that I've carried with me my whole life.

The fear of abandonment is what keeps most people from expressing themselves, and I am no exception. Usually, we are so worried about our partner(s) leaving us for someone else or judging us that we can't even enjoy and love each other in the first place. For relationships in which couples openly practice BDSM, however, I see the complete opposite. These couples are so honest and loving with their partner(s) that the fear factor is minuscule, if not completely gone, and is replaced by love. That can only start with a foundation of trust.

I'm not suggesting that women should go home tonight dressed in full dominatrix wear, or that men should sit down at the dinner table in a bra and panties out of the blue, but why not take a step toward authenticity in a safe and non-threatening way with yourself and your partner(s), whatever form that might take?

Becoming a professional dominatrix brought about positive effects in every area of my life, both personally and professionally. It gave me a new perspective on what was actually scary and what wasn't, which enabled me to become a bigger risk-taker.

I've also gained a brand new understanding of respect. You know the oft-spoken business mantra, "The customer is always right?" That's a huge load of un-empowering crap. If I act like a professional, I deserve respect from my client. Before my work in BDSM, I didn't expect respect in return for my dedication. Now, I demand it.

One of my favorite things to do when a client shows up late is to rope his cock and balls up towards his abdomen for full exposure. Once everything is secure, I duct tape him to the wall in an X position and leave the room. I return armed with a sturdy plastic bow and arrow set.

"Well, you know Mistress is athletic, so let's see how well I aim," I say. As I raise the bow and pull back the arrow, aiming at the sub's cock and balls, I ask, "Are you going to be late again?"

"No Mistress," he says, and I shoot and hit his abdomen.

"This is fun," I say, "let me try again." I pull back the arrow. "Are you going to be late again?" I ask.

"No Mistress," he says. I hit his upper thigh...

This continues until I actually hit the target or get tired of picking up the arrows. After I release the sub, he must give me body worship that includes a foot and leg massage to show his sincere regret for his tardiness.

During sessions, the sub is not permitted to speak to me unless I give him permission. He is allowed to respond briefly to any questions I ask ("Yes, Mistress, No, Mistress") or he may ask for "mercy" (typically, this is a safe word used to opt out of the session if he is uncomfortable with the play for any reason). In this way, the punishments for tardiness and other infractions—no matter how extreme they may seem—stay completely within the bounds of what we are both comfortable with.

THEN AND NOW

I realize that it's unacceptable to most people in the real world to duct tape and punish someone for being late, and of course I would never react that way outside of work. I do, however, see it as a waste of my time and feelings when other people act inconsiderately toward me. Once someone shows me more than once who they are by disrespecting my time and feelings, I don't go back for more. This now applies to every area of my life and is an incredible improvement from where I was—overly accommodating and self-sacrificing to a harmful degree—just a few years ago.

When I was running my wellness studio, there was a part of me that felt I didn't deserve the money that I was making. I felt like it was my responsibility to make potential clients "a deal" no matter what. I always answered, "yes," when asked whether my fees were negotiable because I believed that sticking to my fees would make me lose the business. Wasn't some money better than no money?

In essence, I was projecting to the world, "I am willing to work like a dog. And I am willing to work like a dog for very little money. I am willing to do this because I don't deserve 'real wealth,' so I will settle for whatever I'm offered."

When I started to take charge of my own life, I began by putting different energy out into the Universe, specifically in regard to money. I decided there was no way I was going back to my old tired ways of thinking and believing. I started believing that money flows effortlessly to me, and that my supply is continuously replaced according to my needs and desires.

Going to work in The Dungeon, surrounded by women who wouldn't hesitate to spit in a client's face and then tear apart his wallet if he disrespected their worth, definitely helped me change my ways. I remember hearing the Head Mistress on the phone with a client discussing his appointment. Just before she hung up, she yelled into the phone, "And don't forget to bring the money!" I loved it! It was so refreshing to be working with a group of women who don't take any shit from anyone, and who know their self-worth.

These days, I only put positive thoughts about my acceptance and relationship with wealth and money out into the Universe. I don't overwork myself because I realize money is continually replaced and I don't need to stress over income. I let go of my fears about wealth, and I gave up caring what other people think of me and my income. Most important of all, though, I will no longer allow anyone to devalue me. If a potential client contacts me and asks if my expected "tribute" is negotiable, I don't hesitate to eliminate that person from my life immediately.

GROWING PAINS

If a family member, boyfriend, or friend hurts my feelings or disrespects me, I call them out on it and expect them to do the same with me. Furthermore, I'm willing to risk having arguments, even if it means I might lose the relationship altogether. I figure that if the relationship is worth it for both us, it can hold up to growth, change, honesty, and even occasional conflict. If not, I've found that taking time and redirecting focus are the best ways to wade through the moving-on and letting-go process.

It is difficult for many of us to put in our feelings and desires first—to be "selfish." This isn't easy for me either. In creating the life I now love by making choices that work for me, I know that I sometimes hurt other people who don't understand or approve of my decisions. I am saddened by the loss of my old life and my old relationships that no longer contribute to my happiness, but I am reassured by the knowledge that I am shaping my reality into exactly what I need it to be.

It is my belief that, through the Law of Attraction, we all constantly attract reflections of ourselves. We find people who are like us, in obvious and subtle ways, no matter how blissful or miserable we may be. Others may be guided into our physical reality to help us move toward the Truth, but ultimately it is our own thoughts and feelings that manifest our lives. I can no longer look outside of myself for the cause of my failed personal or professional relationships. I have to become what I am seeking. If I desire relationships with others who are available emotionally, physically, and spiritually, then I have to become those things.

God gives us everything we desire—as long as we don't resist what we want in the same breath we're asking for it.

WHAT MATTERS MOST

The hardest decision for me to make, though, is always the decision to end a romantic relationship with someone, when we have chemistry together but nothing deeper. Working in the BDSM industry, though, has slowly changed my perspective on this topic as well: I have come to understand that healthy, lasting relationships are about a lot more than just good chemistry.

Not long ago, I was sitting in Barnes and Noble with a new photographer, discussing the possibility of our working together. I wanted to be honest with him about my spiritual journey and publishing my book. I wasn't sure about how risqué the cover photo should be, and since he and I would be manifesting the photo together, I wanted to be sure that this would not be an issue for him.

As I told him my story and the details of the book, the photographer was fascinated and intrigued. He asked me about my personal relationships with my clients. "How do you manage not to get emotionally evolved with your clients? I would guess you can't put any emotions into your work."

I smiled. "Actually, I use all my emotions and energy in my work. I just don't get confused about the nature of my relationship with my clients."

All the uplifting and euphoric chemicals in our brain that spin through our systems when we feel respected and admired are similar to what it feels like when we are in love, and that can be very confusing working in this industry. Most websites catering to professionals in this industry loudly advise, "Don't date clients!" The reasoning behind this admonishment is that the client doesn't really know us personally, and once the session is over, the relationship is over. That's it. Walk away.

Interestingly, all the professional women I've spoken to about this topic agree with me. We prefer to session with married men for this very reason—to avoid chemistry confusion.

I'm not suggesting that chemistry isn't important when working with a client. In fact, if I session with a client once and we have no chemistry, I don't see him again. The whole point of the transmutation of sexual energy is to manifest positive influences in my life. I don't want to be putting out low vibrations into the Universe and creating my physical reality of people, places, and things out of the same low vibration. The same holds true in my personal life.

BDSM has taught me that while sexual chemistry is exciting and beneficial, it is not the only component of a loving personal relationship. Just as I can recognize that my professional relationships with clients are fantasies that begin and end in the length of a session, I now recognize the fantasies in my personal relationships, and understand the paramount importance of deep, mutual respect. Now, I ask myself, *Will I still want to be here after the fantasy I created about this person in my mind is over?* and if the answer is no, then I am confident enough to walk away.

WHO'S COUNTING? NOT ME.

⤚

I can't even begin to count the ways I am grateful for all the help I received from everyone at The Dungeon—from the owner, Head Mistresses, Mistresses, house workers, and even the slaves for ball-busting training—but after working there for just a few short months, I had the opportunity to show them my gratitude.

One afternoon I heard Head Mistress Barbara scream my name from the parlor, "Viv!" I eased out of my lounge chair and walked over to her desk. "What's up?" I asked.

"Viv, we have two new Mistresses, and I was hoping you would train them on using a bullwhip?" I couldn't believe it! I had crossed over to the other side! Instead of being the inexperienced and intimidated new Mistress, I was now the veteran passing my experience on to others!

All my passion for teaching and educating surfaced, and from that moment on, I took every opportunity to give back what was given to me. There wasn't a day that went by that I didn't help new the Mistresses train or answer their questions. The women were great; I can't remember ever having more fun at a job. Teaching them the ins and outs of the job and getting to know them personally was an incredibly rewarding experience. At lunch or between clients, we talked about our hopes and dreams, guys and girls, our personal projects, and the Domme business. Some of best times were when a new Mistress would bring a slave client into the lounge for humiliation in front of the whole group. It certainly livened up an afternoon! There is never a dull moment at the Dungeon.

It's funny now to look back at how scared I was, walking for the first time into a subculture of BDSM and domination and submission, but I am glad every day that I found the courage to walk down those dark and dirty stairs on that first day. In my time as a professional dominatrix, I have met some of the most amazing, confident women I've ever known. Even the scary Head Mistress. One young Mistress of about 25 put it best when she told me and the other Mistresses, "I am so amazed by all of you. Your positive impact will influence my self-confidence for the rest of my life."

At The Dungeon, we Mistresses are an eclectic group. Besides all of our different sexual preferences, we all have different dreams and desires as well. One woman is finishing her Ph.D., and one woman is a film producer. There's an aspiring photographer, a classical musician, a painter, an opera singer, and a holistic practitioner, too.

Like the young 25-year-old, I too will be inspired by these women and this experience my entire life. No longer do I judge or make assumptions about people. The dark and stormy night of my interview was the beginning of my transformation into a more loving, compassionate, trusting, curious, playful, confident person. Tantra taught me about my relationship with myself, but BDSM taught me about relationships with others.

Chapter Ten

RETURNING TO AN ABOVEGROUND LIFE

———◦◦◦———

"Faith is taking the first step even when
you don't see the whole staircase."

~MARTIN LUTHER KING JR.

After a year at The Dungeon, it was time for me to take my lessons learned and move on—to leave the safety of The Dungeon and create the life I dreamed of. It all seems so crazy and wild to me. I went from working in the wellness field to embarking on a completely unexpected adventure as a dominatrix, and now I'm manifesting my dreams of becoming an author and inspirational speaker. When my journey began four years ago, I had no idea that I would end up here; I assumed I'd be writing and maybe speaking locally about healthy holistic life choices. Little did I know the Universe had something else in mind for me.

I decided to use all my entrepreneurial skills to work as an independent dominatrix, which gave me time to sit down at my computer and write about my journey into the subculture of BDSM, and already, this new phase of my life has been filled with an abundance of love, joy, good health, compassion, nature, and prosperity.

Nevertheless, fear found an opportunity to rear its ugly head, as it always does eventually.

It was one thing being safe and secure in The Dungeon with a routine and a steady income, but now working as an independent Domme, I had a thousand decisions to make. I had to figure out where I would offer my sessions, what my expected tribute would be, and where to advertise.

After days of contacting BDSM studios and dungeons in NYC, I found out that their thinking process wasn't much different than in the salon industry. They did not want independent Dommes coming into their establishment and stealing away their submissive clients and house slaves. This was an unforeseen hurdle that I needed to figure out. I needed to start thinking differently and taking risks if I wanted to succeed, and I thought to myself, Who do I know that's connected and an influencer in the BDSM community?

About six months prior to leaving The Dungeon, I attended a "Fire Play" workshop at one of the popular "playgrounds" in New York City. One of the other experienced Dommes I worked with at the time introduced me to the modality while we were relaxing in the Mistress lounge.

"Hey Vivian," she'd said, "I've been looking at the fetish workshops coming up, and I'd really love to learn Fire Play."

"What the hell is Fire Play?" I responded.

She clued me in: "It's when the Top uses fire torches across the sub's body and applies fire cups to their skin." That sounded a little scary and dangerous to me. I was all in.

We got there early to be sure we'd get a seat in the front aisle. The stage was set up with a massage table, a working table that held all the torches, containers of alcohol, and glass cups (like those an acupuncturist uses). Off to the side, I saw a fire extinguisher and fire blanket.

The gentleman Fire Play expert finally entered the stage and began to explain the equipment, the benefits of playing with fire, and safety guidelines of the practice. Afterwards, his naked female sub was allowed to join him on stage. She was petite, with a small frame and breasts. Her Master lit the torches and proceeded to run streams of fire down the woman's back, butt, and legs. It was quite a show. The lights in the auditorium were dimmed and streams of fire filled the stage.

It was only when he switched to the glass fire cups that I started feeling freaked out.

One by one, he filled the cups with fire and placed them on this sub's naked body. The cup formed a suction action that lifted the sub's skin and flesh up inside, causing it to turn deep red from the blood being drawn upwards. It was fascinating in a disturbing kind of way, but it piqued my curiosity, and after the two-hour workshop, I mingled and introduced myself to the organizer of the playground and we exchanged our contact information. This conversation came in handy six months later when I needed advice and a referral on where I could start sessioning once I left The Dungeon. After a few emails back and forth, he referred me to an upscale and discreet Midtown studio where I found a new home.

The new BDSM studio was great! It was a smaller space than The Dungeon, but that made it all the more interesting and gave it a feel of a closer community. It was owned and operated by a woman who had been in the fetish and BDSM industry for 20 years.

It also had a completely different setup than I was used to at The Dungeon. When I was there I worked for someone, whereas all of the women at the new studio were independent dominatrixes and fetishists. This system is perfect. The owner has our profiles up on her website, and when you click the photo of the Domme you'd like to session with, you're directed to her professional website, and that's where the communication starts. Once we have a session arranged, we go onto a shared Google calendar and schedule a room rental. The owner was understanding if we had to cancel a room at the last minute and never charged us for this space.

This setup also eliminated the intense competition and envy between the women that was sometimes a problem at The Dungeon. It was more of a supportive environment. I remember sitting around one day having a positive conversation with a group of us from all different backgrounds and cultures. There was me, the middle aged white woman, a young black guy, a young corporate white guy, and a young Hispanic woman. We all got into a conversation about the benefits and the mind/body/spirit healing that we'd discovered through BDSM, and we were all in agreement that this practice is a form of meditation. It was so incredibly natural and awesome to have the experience of being around like-minded people.

It was also very freeing to be able to socialize with the clients after a session. The Dungeon had strict rules about our socializing with clients outside of a session, but being an independent meant if I felt like having a wonderful dinner in Manhattan after a session, I could do so. It was awesome!

FINDING THE WORDS
TO TELL MY STORY

O nce my work was secure, I had to decide about bringing my story out of the dark and into the light. I had already started to write and edit Switch before I left The Dungeon, but I had no idea about the steps I'd need to take to complete the project and to reinvent myself as an author and expert in my new field: an expert in bridging the gap between sexuality and a lifestyle that focuses on holistic health of the mind, body, and spirit. Here I was again, assessing my situation.

- I'm 56 years old.

- I no longer have any connections in the wellness industry.

- I still have no financial savings.

- I've been practically living underground for a year.

- I'm a NYC dominatrix.

- I'm scared about coming out into the light.

The first thing I decided was that if I wanted to go through with writing a book about my journey from holistic practitioner to professional dominatrix, it was going to be an exceptional product. I had to create it the best I could.

Once again the Universe aliened perfectly to help me.

Over about a week's time, I kept stumbling across a writer's blog that mentioned how a particular editor had turned his book from "Chicken shit to chicken salad." I was impressed by how the writer opened up about his lack of editing skills for the world to see. I trusted him and decided to email the editor mentioned in the blog to see if he'd be interested in editing my work. After all, I wanted chicken salad too.

This was not easy for me. I was very intimidated to approach him, but I knew that other than writing wellness articles, I had no publishing experience. I kept thinking, If the professional blogger's manuscript was chicken shit, what does that make mine? I had to let my pride go and suck it up. I explained in my email that I'd already had two different editors work on the project, but I felt that one more set of eyes would help. He got back to me in two days, and we set up a phone meeting the following Monday.

In the meantime I started thinking, What if this guy's a Mormon or something? I can't get on the phone with him and just blurt out that I'm a dominatrix and start telling him BDSM dungeon stories. So I decided to email him on Sunday night before our meeting and give him the elevator pitch: "Before we speak tomorrow, I want to give you a heads up about my book. I'm a holistic practitioner who lost everything and became a NYC dominatrix at 55 year old." Fifteen minutes later I received his response: "Wonderful Sandra, we'll talk tomorrow."

The phone conversation was awkward to say the least. The first two editors were women, so this was the first time I'd actually disclosed my secret life and activities to a man. I briefly described my journey and the process of the book's development for him. He listened without judgment while I spoke, and at the end I said, "Coming out with my story could be a shit show. I'm going to be stirring up a lot of emotions from people," and he agreed, adding, "There are shit shows and there are shit shows. Your show could be really good."

We decided to move forward and let the show begin. Little did I know at the time, our act together would last for months. Honestly, I thought the first couple drafts of the manuscript were decent and I didn't expect the notes and edits I received back! I went into shock! I couldn't even go through the material right away. His notes were all in caps, and regardless of what he'd actually written, I read each one as "WHAT ARE YOU, A FUCKING IDIOT?!" I needed to step back, breathe, and accept the changes I needed to make.

I was humbled, but also grateful that he didn't wash his hands of the whole deal. It was exactly how I felt the first day of work at The Dungeon when the scary Head Mistress cussed me out as soon as I walked in the door.

I admit, working with the editor wasn't easy on many levels. I had to really let go and trust his advice, talent, and experience. I remember one of his regular statements to me was "Quit telling me, and start showing me." For the longest time, I had no idea what he was talking about, and we had to set up a phone meeting specifically to talk about it. I used to get so frustrated about learning "to show and not tell" that I started adding the phrase into my BDSM sessions. As I was punishing my 'school-aged boy' with a spanking, washing his mouth out with soap, or making him stand in the corner for misbehaving, he'd always claim, "Mommy, I'm sorry. I'll be a good boy, I promise." After working with this editor, my comeback became "Well, you better stop telling me, and start showing me!" (It was highly therapeutic.)

Besides having to learn to create and write a full-length book, the project was also emotionally and physically challenging.

I'm a very active person and having been an entrepreneur for 20 years, I was always surrounded by a lot of people. During this two-year process, I was very isolated and sedentary, which took a toll on me. I sat on my couch with a laptop on my lap for basically two years. There are physical holes in the fabric of my sofa where my calves rested on it, and I gained 20 pounds. Recently I was listening to an interview with Tony Robbins about his new book about finance. The interviewer asked him why it's been 20 years since he wrote his last book, and Tony's answer was that he didn't want to physically sit down and write it. I have learned that there will always be steps in creating a project that I'm going to love, but that there will also be steps that I am not excited to climb.

After the manuscript was completely edited and I was free from the sofa seat, I hired a personal trainer to take off the 20 pounds I had gained. I kept the holey sofa.

At that point, I really started to feel free and excited about moving forward on my project, although I had to take care of the final polishing of the manuscript. Piece of cake! I thought, until I started to reach out to copy editors. Wow, did I have a rude awakening!

All three of my content editors had been very supportive and nonjudgmental of me so far, but I was shocked to discover that the copy editors wanted nothing to do with me. Time after time I kept hearing the same thing: "I don't edit this type of material." With every rejection, I found myself baffled, wondering, Are we really still so hung up about sexuality in this country that we can't even be around it, talk about it, and write about it?

I didn't quit, though, and kept reaching out until one day I found a young woman who was willing to take a look at my material. She turned out to be such a blessing for my business. Not only does she do the meticulous editing for all of my content, she also brings all her passion for writing and creating into my copy. It's so amazing how the universe winds up everything so perfectly--all those other copy editors turned me down so that I could find my perfect match. Now, more than a year later, we're still working closely together.

Okay, so now I had a polished manuscript. Now what? I needed advice, so I reached out to my friend John (the guy and businessman who recommended me using my sexual energy in the interview). I met him at his office on a Thursday evening after his staff clocked out. I was feeling very tense, and John felt my tension immediately when he gave me a hug hello. "What's wrong? You're as stiff as a board! What happened?" he said. I started at the beginning.

"Oh my god," he said when I finished. "This is one hell of a story. Let's go eat and talk about it."

The first thing John asked me at dinner was "How's your social media? How many followers do you have on Facebook?" I hadn't really thought about it before. I was on Facebook, but mostly to have fun with friends or talk about health and wellbeing. I answered "about 250 friends." John just laughed. "That's embarrassing! You need to start building up your social media followers and presence if you want to sell a book. Starting tomorrow, you're going to send out requests for friends, and I'm going to help you with referrals."

A NETWORK OF IDEAS

Slowly but surely, I started developing my social media outlets and connecting and networking through Facebook, Twitter, LinkedIn, Instagram, Google +, and YouTube. I was still reluctant at first, nervous about coming clean about my life switch to everyone who could see my online profiles. I could still have posts about health, wellness, and the mind/body/spirit connection, but now I had to add sexuality in the mix.

I brought it into my online presence little by little...and little by little, my followers and friends started dropping away. The one thing that I have learned over the last four years is that not everyone is going to relate to what I have to say, and that's okay. When I went to work as a dominatrix, I lost many friends and colleagues, but there are many new friends and colleagues who took their places and support me no matter what.

It took a while, but I learned not to take it personally. Everyone has free will to choose who they want in their lives. Working as a dominatrix gave me courage to be authentic no matter what, which is something I will not let go of. It's okay for some people not to understand the choices we make.

I was ready to go public.

A female sexuality empowerment blogger happened to see one of my photos on Twitter and reached out to me to do an interview. That was the start of something big. Here is the interview:

Sandra LaMorgese's life trajectory, and her experience of her boudoir shoot, is the embodiment of this blog's mission. She's glorious proof that mature women are vital, sensual, sexual beings capable of transforming their lives at a stage when the traditionalist culture tells us we're "over." Sandra's story echoes Eleanor Roosevelt's clarion call to every woman who doubts herself: "you must do the thing you think you cannot do."

At the age of 55, I decided to step out of my box from being a Holistic Practitioner to being a Professional Dominatrix and Fetishist. At the time, I was convinced that this switch was an improbability due to my age. However, as ridiculous as it all sounded to me, I felt this experience would empower me personally and professionally, and help me get in touch with my sexuality.

Surprisingly, upon entering the subculture of BDSM, I soon discovered that my mature image, confidence, life experience, and "chill" were not a detriment to my success — in fact, my mature attributes were beneficial.

My feeling is, women are beautiful and sexy at every age and every stage of life. Was it effortless for me to get comfortable looking at revealing photographs of myself over 50? No, it was not. I had to change my thoughts, beliefs, and feelings about what is beautiful, sexy, and desirable to me. Once that happened, I was like, "I got this!"

Once I shared this interview on my social networks and received positive reinforcement, I started getting more confident. I had stuck my toe in the water to feel the temperature, and it was fine.

After that first interview, other like-minded women started asking me for interviews, and we started supporting one another publicly by sharing our articles, blogs, and products. I started my own podcast and started interviewing them. We started to lift each other up in a world where women are misunderstood more often than not when they discuss sexuality. We all found ourselves enduring the same things: sexual comments via private messages, cock shots sent to us by strangers, haters by the hundreds making comments on our social media accounts about how sick we for discussing sex, sex toys, fetishes, BDSM, orgasms, and displaying our sexy photos. The truth is, every one of us was respectful to others and to ourselves. We were working passionately to empower other women to feel good and excited about their sexuality, regardless of their desires, orientations, or preferences. Sometimes, I just had to laugh to myself and think, I really wish I was having as much sex as everyone thought I was. I'm sitting home at night like everyone else watching The Golden Girls. Beyond the negativity that I (still) receive on the Internet and in person, it's the positive reinforcement that keeps me motivated. Every time a woman or man emails me to thank me for my courage and authenticity, I get lifted up. This is where I find my strength and motivation to continue.

When I finally decided that I was ready for real change, I was feeling really good about who I was, who I wanted to become, and how I wanted to inspire others. I decided that the only way to continue evolving was to take bigger risks. I had learned to walk the walk and talk the talk, and now I was ready to tell the world about it!

Chapter Eleven

JOINING THE
CONVERSATION

———⟨⟩———

"We delight in the beauty of the butterfly, but rarely admit the changes it has gone through to achieve that beauty."

~MAYA ANGELO

The more I branched out, the more I stopped relying on my limited perspective. I began to see that everything was woven together perfectly to help me express the highest authenticity of myself. I just needed to trust it.

STEP BY STEP

⟨⟩

When one of my blogger friends asked me if I was willing to do a photo shoot with the Huffington Post, I obviously jumped at the opportunity. The shoot showcased women over 50 who showed their un-retouched thighs. I had been on quite a few photo shoots in my life, so I was very relaxed about it. It wasn't as if they were looking for a 20 year-old woman with perfect legs, and I believe that at my age, my legs look pretty nice. In any case, I figured this was just going to be a 15-minute photo shoot that I would be able to post on my social networks to show that I had worked with the Huffington Post on a fun project.

When I arrived at the AOL building in Manhattan, I signed in and they directed me to the appropriate floor. I took a seat on the sofa, and the woman in charge of the shoot gave me a model release form to sign and told me she would be with me shortly. As instructed, I had brought along a little black T-shirt and short black shorts.

When everything was ready for me on the shoot, I ducked behind a banner and changed into my little outfit next to a wall covered in actor headshots. One of them was Ethan Hawke, whom I totally have a crush on. When the photographer was ready, I walked over, and the entire ordeal took less than 15 minutes, as they'd promised. I got back behind the screen, changed into my jeans, blew Ethan a kiss goodbye, and left.

About two weeks later I received an email from the woman at The Huffington Post thanking me for participating in the shoot and giving me a link to the live article. To be honest, I wasn't crazy about my photo. The photos were unedited, and the one they used of my thighs were of me sitting on a stool with my legs intertwined. Hence, major cellulite.

I decided I could live with cellulite photo--that was, after all, the point of the shoot-- but I no longer felt the need to share the post on my social networks. In my limited perspective, I felt like the shoot had been a good experience, but mostly a waste of my time professionally, and I was glad the whole ordeal was over. I emailed the manager back, thanked her for inviting me, congratulated her on an excellent article, and then put the whole experience out of my mind.

Then a funny thing happened.

I went to a nude beach.

It was an impulsive decision, but I was looking for new ways to freshen up my life and my thinking, and I decided that trying something completely new would be a good way to give me a mental and emotional boost. After I went, I wrote about it for my personal blog:

"I'm 59 years old—I am not going to a nude beach."

Two of my close friends had been asking me to come with them to their favorite nude beach for months, and each time they asked, I gave them this same answer.

I had never been to a nude beach before, and I was happy to let that trend continue. It wasn't because I hate my body or am hung up about sexuality—on the contrary, I'm in good shape and when it comes to sexuality, I am more than willing to take risks and try new things.

A nude beach, though, just sounded uncomfortable. Getting soaked and naked with large groups of strangers was an activity I had no interest in whatsoever. Not only was I not willing to take the risk of exposing myself, I surely didn't want to be a witness of some naked guy bending over to grab a volleyball. I couldn't fathom why my friends wanted to have such experiences.

After turning down their invitations for months and months, however, curiosity got the best of me. I had to figure out why they loved it so much. And, because I regularly write and speak on topics like self-esteem, sexuality, and empowerment, I decided to bring along my photographer to document this first-time experience. I was willing to share my journey, whether it turned out positive or negative.

When we arrived at Sandy Hook beach, the first surprise was how calm and secluded it was. This was not the typical Jersey shore—there were no wild parties, no vendors, no blaring music, and no bling.

The second surprise was the variety of people present. On the whole beach, I could see only one supermodel-type, and the rest were just regular people with regular bodies, from their early twenties up in to their seventies. The majority were middle aged. Some people had tattoos, but most seemed pretty vanilla. This was not a beach full of wild, sex-crazed swingers or perfectly toned and tanned workout goddesses—these were just normal people, enjoying the sun, the waves, and the sand, just without bathing suits.

So I joined them.

I stripped off everything and walked off toward the shoreline with my photographer. As he snapped off photos of me near the surf, I felt my insecurities about body image and exposing my private parts start to fade away. All the years of my misperceptions about what other people thought of my naked body disappeared. All my scars and stretch marks that told my life story took on a badge of honor, instead of the shame game I had been playing with myself all those years.

After the photos, we put away the camera, flapped out our towels on the sand, and sprayed on sunscreen like there was no tomorrow. At this point, I started looking around, taking in the people and the atmosphere of the nude beach. What I felt and saw in those minutes, relaxing on the sun-warmed sand, made me feel silly for worrying so much earlier that morning.

No one seemed uncomfortable. No one was staring at other beach-goers' bodies or rubbernecking to see if people were staring back at them. No one was trying to hide or flaunt anything, so there was no reason for anyone to gawk.

That day on the nude beach, though, no one was judging, even though many sunbathers there had stretch marks, aged skin, and cellulite.

The longer I spent on that sunny judgment-free afternoon, the more I felt light, free, and relaxed. I even chatted, still completely bare, with fellow sunbathers and a cute park ranger. No one else seemed interested about their bodies or mine, it was all about feeling free of the stigma of body image and enjoying the ocean, sun, and the wildlife.

I was so sure that I never wanted to visit a nude beach before I tried it, but now feel like I never want to go back to a non-nude beach again. Allowing myself to be so vulnerable empowered me.

GAINING MOMENTUM

The whole experience had been just as fun and refreshing as I hoped it would be, and I wanted to share it with the world, so I reached out to my blogger friend and asked her if she'd be interested in interviewing me about the experience. "That's an awesome idea Sandra, I would love to interview you for my blog, she responded. Great! I thought, and I sent her a few photos. But while I was waiting that weekend for the questions to arrive from her, I had an inspirational thought: If my friend thought it was such a great idea, maybe other people would too. So I sat down at my computer and emailed the lady from the Huffington Post photo shoot:

Hi Becky,

I'm reaching out to see if you'd be interested in interviewing me about 'why and how' going to a nude beach for the first at age 59 (no makeup or hair done) empowered me. Of course, I took my photographer with me :)

Best,

Sandra

That Monday, I received an email from her saying how she'd love to hear more and that she was going to loop me in with the editor at HuffPost50! WOW, I thought, This is going to be a great interview. A few hours later I received an email from the editor at HuffPost50 inviting me to write an entire blog post about the experience and offering me my own blogging profile. I couldn't believe it, I wasn't expecting anything so phenomenal! I'd expected a two-paragraph interview with someone over at The Huffington Post, but little did I know that a 15 minute photo shoot of my thighs would lead me into the potential of millions of views on The Huffington Post.

As soon as I finished reading her email, I called Jessica, my copy editor. Even before I could tell her what had happened, she knew something was up--I always text or email, but I was way too excited to wait. "Sandra, what's going on?" she asked, and after I told her the whole story, we spent the next four hours writing and editing the article. I submitted it to my new Huffington Post profile that same day and waited, anxious and eager, for something to happen.

And something did happen!

When the article went live, I watched the activity of shares and likes like a hawk, and I read and responded to all the supportive comments. As the day went on, I watched the stats rising higher and higher: 200, 300, 400... 1000, 2000 3000.... By the end of the day, the blog had over 7000 shares and likes. I even tried to post the article on Reddit, but was refused because the article had already been shared so many times.

I had taken a really big risk by going to the nude beach that day and by going public with my story, but it totally paid off for me personally and professionally.

CREATING SANDRA LAMORGESE, PHD

After the nude beach article settled down, I went back into my Huffington Post blogger profile to find out exactly what I could and could not write about, and discovered that I could write about anything I wanted. This scared me a little, or maybe a lot. Out of nowhere, I had the chance to have a loud voice and write authentically. It was a similar feeling to how I felt about going to work as a dominatrix at the BDSM dungeon. I knew I was going to receive massive criticism about the topics I chose to write about, but at the same time, I knew it was my dream come true. For so long, I had hoped to reach out and write authentically about the people, places, and things that I was passionate about, and now an opportunity to do exactly that had landed in my life. It would be tragic, I knew, to walk away or half-ass it just because I was afraid.

I read everything I could find on creating an online presence and a brand. Everything I read said the same thing over and over again: "Playing it safe is the riskiest thing you can do." So, just as I had found myself with a blank canvas in creating Mistress Vivian, I was presented with another blank canvas to create Sandra LaMorgese PhD. And just like that, I forged ahead and trusted that I'd figure out the details along the way.

I knew from the beginning that I wanted to be true to myself. I didn't want to create a fake image or fake persona that would be ridiculous and time-consuming to maintain. Isn't that how Marilyn Monroe got in trouble? I wanted to be me, but bigger. Everything in the media is larger-than-life, and I would have to be too. I had to take risks with how I looked, what I wrote about, and my beliefs.

In addition to being true to myself, I wanted to create material that was relatable, informative, and thought-provoking--and I found out right away that there is a fine line between the three, as when I wrote my article on "Why I Powder and Diaper Powerful, Successful, Middle-Aged Men." The article was posted on my Huffington Post profile as usual, but I quickly realized that while it was informative and thought-provoking, it wasn't even close to relatable. Although there are several adult baby communities with an active online presence, the majority of the readers of the Huffington Post are not a part of them, so instead of hundreds or even thousands of shares, likes, and comments, the article only reached around 50 people.

Clearly, there were many ups and downs involved in the process of developing my new online persona, but like everything else, practice is the key to success.

Along with the content of my articles, I wanted to think of ways that would help my blog stand out from the rest. The first person that came to my mind was Oprah Winfrey. Every time I went to the grocery store and saw the "O" Magazine on the rack, I couldn't help but notice that the only person who on the cover every month was Oprah Winfrey. Not everyone is a huge Oprah Winfrey fan, I think we can all agree that she's a marketing genius, so I adopted her as a branding role model. Instead of using stock photography for my articles, I began reaching out to professional photographers who were interested in having their art featured on The Huffington Post and driving traffic back to their website. I also started reaching out to other interesting, passionate, and visionary people to profile in my articles.

Just like that, I was getting a lot of people interested in coming on board and creating these projects, and I was developing a reputation for excellence and getting things done. Before I knew it people started contacting me through my social networks and website email asking if they could be part of my projects. People were starting to trust me, and the momentum we were creating together was exciting for all of us.

But of course, there were obstacles.

A NEW KIND OF PUSHBACK

Please get yourself some in-depth psychotherapy. There's something deeply wrong with the way you think."

Wow, my first hate mail! I had mixed feelings about it, since I really didn't feel I needed psychotherapy, but I decided not to take it personally. It was one person's opinion and they were entitled to it. Plus, it made me feel like I had made it in the contentious world of online media.

The article (which I've included below) that made this woman so emotional was titled, "Swinging Is Back, But Is It Right For You?" Remember stories from the 60s and 70s, when couples went to parties and put their house keys in a punch bowl? The person's keys you drew at the end of the night was the person you went home with.

Few people know this, but swinging as a fad in America actually began in the 1950s with Air Force officers in California swapping wives. Today, though, in clubs and private homes in London, Paris, New York, and many other places, the swinger trend has reemerged. Nightline, ABC News, The Daily Mail and plenty of other media outlets have covered it. Some participants are bored, middle-aged couples trying to revitalize their sex lives. Others are young, sophisticated urbanites looking for a weekend thrill and a way to blow off steam after a stressful work week.

Times have certainly changed since the 60s Sexual Revolution! What was once extremely taboo and only took place behind closed doors now has a website, and researchers are noticing a shift toward younger generations. Once, swingers were generally 35+, but that's changing. Today's twenty- and thirty-somethings are marrying later and are taking their liberated dating habits into marriage, so it's not surprising that they are also more apt to take part in zestier enterprises once there, lacking the urge for secrecy and guilt the older generation faced.

Gen X and Millennials are interpreting monogamy in an entirely new way these days. What's more, women seem to be the ones driving the most recent swinging fad, calling the shots and being choosy with their partners.

So should you try swinging? That's entirely up to you, your partner, and your shared interpretation of your relationship. Some people can't stand the idea of their lover with someone else. Others find nothing hotter. There are women who allow their partner to kiss and touch other partners, but still keep sex off-limits. Others allow kissing, touching and oral sex, but no penetration. Some couples allow freebies during business trips or when one partner is more than 20 miles away from home. Then, of course, there are plenty of "no holds barred" couples as well. There are endless variations and combinations. Some couples don't want to know anything about the other's escapades; others want to know every detail. Swingers are just as varied and individual as any like minded group of people, and it all comes down to individual preferences that have been clearly communicated between committed partners.

So how can you get into swinging? If this is a conversation you've never had with your partner, try to feel them out first with indirect questions and casual conversation. Be subtle at first. Suggest a movie or book where swinging takes place and is portrayed positively, and then see how they react. Then sometime later discuss it with them, and don't just make it sound like you're looking for some guilt-free cheating. Tell them what excites you and turns you on about it, and ask if it excites them too.

Never pressure anyone into taking part, and never accept being pressured. Everyone deserves sovereignty over their own body and emotional boundaries. Plus, everyone loves and enjoys sex in their own unique ways. You'll need to discuss at length where each of your boundaries are and establish ground rules about what is acceptable and what goes over the line for each of you.

Start slowly. Perhaps just visit a local event or club and observe. Talk about it afterward: what you noticed, what turned you on, and what didn't. Keep the conversations low-pressure, and try not to take yourselves too seriously. Think of it as a new adventure, and keep an open mind.

If you want to remain in a monogamous relationship, you both have to communicate well, take things slowly, allow time to adjust, be comfortable enough with each other to voice concerns when you are uncomfortable, and support one another throughout the whole process. If it isn't done right, it could damage the relationship, but if both of you are honest, supportive, loving, and understanding, then it can be an exciting, erotic, and rejuvenating experience."

The woman who sent me hate mail, I soon learned, was not alone in her strong feelings. The Huff Post readers went crazy! Apparently, I was damaging the foundation of American marriage and people were not happy to hear about it. On the other hand, I had hundreds of new subscribers to my website that day, more that I have ever received in a single day. That told me that my content really spoke to a large group of people even while it pissed off another group.

MOMENTS OF GROWTH

꿍

I'm like everyone else, in that I want to be liked. It's human nature. But since I've joined the online conversation about wellness and sexuality, I've realized that I need to let that go. People love to make noise on the Internet, and there will always be haters and Internet trolls who show up in the comments sections of my articles. I needed to find a positive angle so that I wouldn't get sucked down into the negativity, so I decided to remember that everyone deserves free will. If exercising that free will meant expressing negativity towards me, then so be it. In addition, I started to accept the controversy and the even to appreciate the back-and-forth banter between the people who supported me and the people who hated me.

I'm not going to lie and say that it's easy, but I do my best to separate myself from the negativity, and that's only possible because I made a decision four years ago that I was going to live in authentic life and be happy no matter what.

CONCLUSION

—⊷—

*"When you are grateful, fear disappears and
abundance appears."*

~ANTHONY ROBBINS

Then, after a year at The Dungeon, it was time for me to take my lessons learned and move on—to leave the safety of The Dungeon and create the life I love. It all seems so crazy and wild to me. I went from working in the wellness field to embarking on an unexpected adventure as a dominatrix, and now I'm manifesting my dreams of becoming an author and inspirational speaker. When my journey began three years ago, I had no idea that I would end up here; I assumed I'd be writing and maybe speaking locally about healthy holistic life choices. Little did I know the Universe had something else in mind for me to write and speak about.

I decided to use all my entrepreneurial skills to work as an independent dominatrix, which gives me time to sit down at my computer and write about my journey into the subculture of BDSM, and already, this new phase of my life has been filled with an abundance of love, joy, good health, compassion, nature, and prosperity.

FROM DESPAIR TO JOY

A fter my studio closed, I remember sitting on my living room floor in a state of despair. I felt utterly purposeless, and I had no idea how to pull myself out of the dark emotional and financial hole that I had somehow fallen into.

Then, as I began experimenting with Tantra, everything I knew about my current reality began to vanish, replaced by a new reality of Divine inspirational thoughts and ideas. I was ready to trust, and as soon as I let go of how I thought my life should be, I started to live my dreams.

I came alive. I was enthusiastic about starting a new life founded in love and not fear. As a dominatrix, I learned to be happy rather than to seek happiness, to experience rather than judge, and to make healthy choices mentally, physically, and spiritually, instead of working myself to death. I started being a friend and family member, instead of isolating myself from others.

I design my life as a part of nature. I am safe and secure. I am free.

I've come a long way since my client David told me about the kinky stories of his cousin and her lady friends. I chalk my prior feelings and beliefs up to my limited perspective and my fear of exploring anything that didn't fit into my comfortable notions of normality.

The most difficult part of my journey was permitting the death of the old me, my old life, and old perspective. I fought for so long to stay in control, and for a while I honestly believed that it was possible to hold on to all the people, places, and things I cared about after my life switch, but it wasn't. Once I made the decision to open myself up to change, I changed. Once that process started, my physical reality changed right along with my thoughts and feelings.

I can't count the number of times (sometimes many times per day) that I tried to walk away from being Mistress Vivian. I lived a double life for so long, as I actively worked to keep my life as a Domme a secret from friends and family members, who I feared would reject me for it. Keeping the secret was exhausting and the stress started to wear me down. I loved my new self, but I was afraid that if I allowed Mistress Vivian into Sandy's vanilla world, the people I cared about would no longer love me.

I feel a very similar fear about publishing this book, stepping into the public sphere and putting myself out there, fully exposed. By bringing my story into the light, though, I hope I am able to help others who are struggling to express their true selves. Becoming a professional dominatrix is not the answer for everyone. Maybe going back to college, opening a new business, coloring your hair green, or taking yoga for the first time is your answer. Maybe it's letting go of shame, guilt, anger, and resentment about who you believe you are and what you desire to become. And maybe, after reading my story, you will think, *If Sandy can overcome her fears, learn to trust, walk into The Dungeon, and enter the extreme subculture of BDSM, maybe*

I can trust too and go for the life of my dreams.

I have been blessed with the courage, faith, and Truth to "walk the walk" with my new way of life, understanding the Truth of who I am, letting go of the negative chatter in my mind, and pursuing the life of my dreams.

Was it easy? Hell no! *Was it worth it?* Oh yes!